Jean Baudrillard

Simulations

Simulations

Jean Baudrillard

Translated by Paul Foss, Paul Patton and Philip Beitchman

Semiotext[e]

Printed in the United States of America

10 9 8 7 6 5 4

Contents

Simulations

The Precession of Simulacra

> The simulacrum is never that which conceals the truth—it is the truth which conceals that there is none.
> The simulacrum is true.

Ecclesiastes

If we were able to take as the finest allegory of simulation the Borges tale where the cartographers of the Empire draw up a map so detailed that it ends up exactly covering the territory (but where the decline of the Empire sees this map become frayed and finally ruined, a few shreds still discernible in the deserts—the metaphysical beauty of this ruined abstraction, bearing witness to an Imperial pride and rotting like a carcass, returning to the substance of the soil, rather as an aging double ends up being confused with the real thing)—then this fable has come full circle for us, and now has nothing but the discrete charm of second-order simulacra. [1]

Abstraction today is no longer that of the map, the double, the mirror or the concept. Simulation is no longer that of a territory, a referential being or a substance. It is the generation by models of a real without origin or reality: a hyperreal. The territory no longer precedes the map, nor survives it. Henceforth, it is the map that precedes the territory — **PRECESSION OF SIMULACRA**—it is the map that engenders the territory and if we were to revive the fable today, it would be the territory whose shreds are slowly rotting across the map. It is the real, and not the map, whose vestiges subsist here and there, in the deserts which are no longer those of the Empire, but our own. *The desert of the real itself.*

In fact, even inverted, the fable is useless. Perhaps only the allegory of the Empire remains. For it is with the same Imperialism that present-day simulators try to make the real, all the real, coincide with their simulation models. But it is no longer a question of either maps or territory. Something has disappeared: the sovereign difference between them that was the abstraction's charm. For it is the difference which forms the poetry of the map and the charm of the territory, the magic of the concept and the charm of the real. This representational imaginary, which both culminates in and is engulfed by the cartographer's mad project of an ideal coextensivity between the map and the territory, disappears with simulation — whose operation is nuclear and genetic, and no longer specular and discursive. With it goes all of metaphysics. No more mirror of being and appearances, of the real and its concept. No more imaginary coextensivity: rather, genetic miniaturisation is the dimension of simulation. The real is produced from miniaturised units, from matrices, memory banks and command models—and with these it can be reproduced an indefinite number of times. It no longer has to be rational, since it is no longer measured against some ideal or negative instance. It is nothing more than operational. In fact, since it is no longer enveloped by an imaginary, it is no longer real at all. It is a hyperreal, the product of an irradiating synthesis of combinatory models in a hyperspace without atmosphere.

In this passage to a space whose

curvature is no longer that of the real, nor of truth, the age of simulation thus begins with a liquidation of all referentials—worse: by their artificial resurrection in systems of signs, a more ductile material than meaning, in that it lends itself to all systems of equivalence, all binary oppositions and all combinatory algebra. It is no longer a question of imitation, nor of reduplication, nor even of parody. It is rather a question of substituting signs of the real for the real itself, that is, an operation to deter every real process by its operational double, a metastable, programmatic, perfect descriptive machine which provides all the signs of the real and short-circuits all its vicissitudes. Never again will the real have to be produced—this is the vital function of the model in a system of death, or rather of anticipated resurrection which no longer leaves any chance even in the event of death. A hyperreal henceforth sheltered from the imaginary, and from any distinction between the real and the imaginary, leaving room only for the orbital recurrence of models and the simulated generation of difference.

The Divine Irreference of Images

To dissimulate is to feign not to have what one has. To simulate is to feign to have what one hasn't. One implies a presence, the other an absence. But the matter is more complicated, since to simulate is not simply to feign: "Someone who feigns an illness can simply go to bed and make believe he is ill. Some who simulates an illness produces in himself some of the symptoms." (Littre) Thus, feigning or dissimulating leaves the reality principle intact: the difference is always clear, it is only masked; whereas simulation threatens the difference between "true" and "false", between "real" and "imaginary". Since the simulator produces. "true" symptoms, is he ill or not? He cannot be treated objectively either as ill, or as not-ill. Psychology and medicine stop at this point, before a thereafter undiscoverable truth of the illness. For if any symptom can be "produced", and can no longer be accepted as a fact of nature, then every illness may be considered as simulatable and simulated, and medicine loses its meaning since it only knows how to treat "true" illnesses by their objective causes. Psychosomatics evolves in a dubious way on the edge of the illness principle. As for psychoanalysis, it transfers the symptom from the organic to the unconscious order: once again, the latter is held to be true, more true than the former— but why should simulation stop at the portals of the unconscious? Why couldn't the "work" of the unconscious be "produced" in the same way as any other symptom in classical medicine? Dreams already are.

The alienist, of course, claims that "for each form of the mental alienation there is a particular order in the succession of symptoms, of which the simulator is unaware and in the absence of which the alienist is unlikely to be deceived." This (which dates from 1865) in order to save at all cost the truth principle, and to escape the spectre raised by simulation—namely that truth, reference and objective causes have ceased to exist. What can medicine do with something which floats on either side of illness, on either side of health, or with the reduplication of illness in a discourse that is no longer true or false? What can psychoanalysis do with the reduplication of the discourse of the unconscious in a discourse of simulation that can never be unmasked, since it isn't false either? [2]

What can the army do with simulators? Traditionally, following a direct principle of identification, it unmasks and punishes them. Today, it can reform an excellent simulator as though he were equivalent to a "real" homosexual, heart-case or lunatic. Even military psychology retreats from the Cartesian clarities and hesitates to draw the distinction between true and false, between the "produced" symptom and the authentic symptom. "If he acts crazy so well, then he must be mad." Nor is it mistaken: in the sense that all lunatics are simulators, and this lack of distinction is the worst form of subversion. Against it classical reason armed itself with all its categories. But it is this today which again outflanks them, submerging the truth principle.

Outside of medicine and the army, favored terrains of simulation, the affair goes back to religion and the simulacrum of divinity: "I forbad any simulacrum in the temples because the divinity that breathes life into nature cannot be represented."

Indeed it can. But what becomes of the divinity when it reveals itself in icons, when it is multiplied in simulacra? Does it remain the supreme authority, simply incarnated in images as a visible theology? Or is it volatilized into simulacra which alone deploy their pomp and power of fascination—the visible machinery of icons being substituted for the pure and intelligible Idea of God? This is precisely what was feared by the Iconoclasts, whose millenial quarrel is still with us today. [3] Their rage to destroy images rose precisely because they sensed this omnipotence of simulacra, this facility they have of effacing God from the consciousness of men, and the overwhelming, destructive truth which they suggest: that ultimately there has never been any God, that only the simulacrum exists, indeed that God himself has only ever been his own simulacrum. Had they been able to believe that images only occulted or masked the Platonic Idea of God, there would have been no reason to destroy them. One can live with the idea of a distorted truth. But their metaphysical despair came from the idea that the images concealed nothing at all, and that in fact they were not images, such as the original model would have made them, but actually perfect simulacra forever radiant with their own fascination. But this death of the divine referential has to be exorcised at all cost.

It can be seen that the iconoclasts, who are often accused of despising and denying images, were in fact the ones who accorded them their actual worth, unlike the iconolaters, who saw in them only reflections and were content to venerate God at one remove. But the converse can also be said, namely that the iconolaters were the most modern and adventurous minds, since underneath the idea of the apparition of God in the mirror of images, they already enacted his death and his disappearance in the epiphany of his representations (which they perhaps knew no longer represented anything, and that they were purely a game, but that this was precisely the greatest game—knowing also that it is dangerous to unmask images, since they dissimulate the fact that there is nothing behind them).

This was the approach of the Jesuits, who based their politics on the virtual disappearance of God and on the worldly and spectacular manipulation of consciences— the evanescence of God in the epiphany of power—the end of transcendence, which no longer serves as alibi for a strategy completely free of influences and signs. Behind the baroque of images hides the grey eminence of politics.

Thus perhaps at stake has always been the murderous capacity of images, muderers of the real, murderers of their own model as the Byzantine icons could murder the divine identity. To this murderous capacity is opposed the dialectical capacity of represent- ations as a visible and intelligible mediation of the Real. All of Western faith and good faith was engaged in this wager on representation: that a sign could refer to the depth of meaning, that a sign could *exchange* for meaning and that something could guarantee this exchange—God, of course. But what if God himself can be simulated, that is to say, reduced to the signs which attest his existence? Then the whole system becomes weightless, it is no longer anything but a gigantic simulacrum—not unreal, but a simulacrum, never again exchanging for what is real, but exchanging in itself, in an uninterrupted circuit without reference or circumference.

So it is with simulation, insofar as it is opposed to representation. The latter starts from the principle that the sign and the real are equivalent (even if this equivalence is utopian, it is a fundamental axiom). Conversely, simulation starts from the *utopia* of this principle of equivalence, *from the radical negation of the sign as value*, from the sign as reversion and death sentence of every reference. Whereas representation tries to absorb simulation by interpreting it as false representation, simulation envelops the whole edifice of representation as itself a simulacrum.

This would be the successive phases of the image:

—it is the reflection of a basic reality

—it masks and perverts a basic reality

—it masks the *absence* of a basic reality

—it bears no relation to any reality whatever: it is its own pure simulacrum.

In the first case, the image is a *good*

appearance—the representation is of the order of sacrament. In the second, it is an *evil* appearance—of the order of malefice. In the third, it *plays at being* an appearance—it is of the order of sorcery. In the fourth, it is no longer in the order of appearance at all, but of simulation.

The transition from signs which dissimulate something to signs which dissimulate that there is nothing, marks the decisive turning point. The first implies a theology of truth and secrecy (to which the notion of ideology still belongs). The second inaugurates an age of simulacra and stimulation, in which there is no longer any God to recognise his own, nor any last judgement to separate true from false, the real from its artificial resurrection, since everything is already dead and risen in advance.

When the real is no longer what it used to be, nostalgia assumes its full meaning. There is a proliferation of myths of origin and signs of reality; of second-hand truth, objectivity and authenticity. There is an escalation of the true, of the lived experience; a resurrection of the figurative where the object and substance have disappeared. And there is a panic-stricken production of the real and the referential, above and parallel to the panic of material production: this is how simulation appears in the phase that concerns us—a strategy of the real, neo-real and hypperral whose universal double is a strategy of deterrence.

Rameses, or Rose-Coloured Resurrection

Ethnology almost met a paradoxical death that day in 1971 when the Phillipino government decided to return the few dozen Tasaday discovered deep in the jungle, where they had lived for eight centuries undisturbed by the rest of mankind, to their primitive state, out of reach of colonists, tourists and ethnologists. This was at the initiative of the anthropologists themselves, who saw the natives decompose immediately on contact, like a mummy in the open air.

For ethnology to live, its object must die. But the latter revenges itself by dying for having been "discovered", and defies by its death the science that wants to take hold of it.

Doesn't every science live on this

paradoxical slope to which it is doomed by the evanescence of its object in the very process of its apprehension, and by the pitiless reversal this dead object exerts on it? Like Orpheus it always turns around too soon, and its object, like Eurydice, falls back into Hades.

It was against this hades of paradox that the ethnologists wanted to protect themselves by cordoning off the Tasaday with virgin forest. Nobody now will touch it: the vein is closed down, like a mine. Science loses a precious capital, but the object will be safe—lost to science, but intact in its "virginity". It isn't a question of sacrifice (science never sacrifices itself: it is always murderous), but of the simulated sacrifice of its object in order to save its reality principle. The Tasaday, frozen in their natural element, provide a perfect alibi, an eternal guarantee. At this point begins a persistent anti-ethnology to which Jaulin, Castaneda and Clastres variously belong. In any case, the logical evolution of a science is to distance itself ever further from its object until it dispenses with it entirely: its autonomy evermore fantastical in reaching its pure form.

The Indian thereby driven back into the ghetto, into the glass coffin of virgin forest, becomes the simulation model for all conceivable Indians *before ethnology*. The latter thus allows itself the luxury of being incarnate beyond itself, in the "brute" reality of these Indians it has entirely reinvented— Savages who are indebted to ethnology for still being Savages: what a turn of events, what a triumph for this science which seemed dedicated to their destruction!

Of course, these particular Savages are posthumous: frozen, cryogenised, sterilised, protected *to death*, they have become referential simulacra, and the science itself a pure simulation. Same thing at Creusot where, in the form of an "open" museum exhibition, they have "museumised" on the spot, as historical witnesses to their period, entire working class quartiers, living metallurgical zones, a complete culture including men, women and children and their gestures, languages and habits—living beings fossilised as in a snap shot. The museum, instead of being curcumscribed in a geometrical location, is now everywhere, like a dimension of life itself. Thus ethnology, now freed from its object, will no longer be circumscribed as an objective science but is applied to all living things and becomes invisible, like an omnipresent fourth dimension, that of the simulacrum. *We are all Tasaday*. or Indians who have once more become "what they used to be", or at least that which ethnology has made them—simulacra Indians who proclaim at last the universal truth of ethnology.

We all become living specimens under the spectral light of ethnology, or of anti-ethnology which is only the pure form of triumphal ethnology, under the sign of dead differences, and of the resurrection of differences. It is thus extremely naive to look for ethnology among the Savages or in some Third World—it is here, everywhere, in the metropolis, among the whites, in a world completely catalogued and analysed and then *artificially revived as though real*, in a world of simulation: of the hallucination of truth, of blackmail by the real, of the murder and historical (hysterical) retrospection of every symbolic form—a murder whose first victims were, noblesse oblige,. the Savages, but which for a long time now has been extended to all Western societies.

But at the same moment ethnology gives up its final and only lesson, the secret which kills it (and which the savages understood much better): the vengeance of the dead.

The confinement of the scientific object is the same as that of the insane and the dead. And just as the whole of society is hopelessly contaminated by that mirror of madness it has held out for itself, so science can only die contaminated by the death of the object which is its inverse mirror. It is science which ostensibly masters the object, but it is the latter which deeply invests the former, following an unconscious reversion, giving only dead and circular replies to a dead and circular interrogation.

Nothing changes when society breaks the mirror of madness (abolishes asylums, gives speech back to the mad, etc.) nor when science seems to break the mirror of its objectivity (effacing itself before its object, as Castaneda does, etc.) and to bow down before "differences". Confinement is succeeded by an apparatus which assumes a countless and endlessly diffractable, multi-pliable form. As fast as ethnology in its classical institution collapses, it survives in an anti-ethnology whose task is to reinject fictional difference and Savagery every-where, in order to conceal the fact that it is this world, our own, which in its way has become savage again, that is to say devastated by difference and death.

It is in this way, under the pretext of saving the original, that the caves of Lascaux have been forbidden to visitors and an exact replica constructed 500 metres away, so that everyone can see them (you glance through a peephole at the real grotto and then visit the reconstituted whole). It is possible that the very memory of the original caves will fade in the mind of future generations, but from now on there is no longer any difference: the duplication is sufficient to render both artificial.

In the same way the whole of science and technology were recently mobilised to save the mummy of Rameses II, after it had been left to deteriorate in the basement of a museum. The West was panic-stricken at the thought of not being able to save what the symbolic order had been able to preserve for 40 centuries, but away from the light and gaze of onlookers. Rameses means nothing to us: only the mummy is of inestimable worth since it is what guarantees that accumulation means something. Out entire linear and accumulative culture would collapse if we could not stockpile the past in plain view. To this end the pharaohs must be brought out of their tombs, and the mummies out of their silence. To this end they must be exhumed and given military honors. They are prey to both science and the worms. Only absolute secrecy ensured their potency throughout the millenia—their mastery over putrefaction, which signified a mastery over the total cycle of exchange with death. *We* know better than to use our science for the *reparation* of the mummy, that is, to restore a *visible* order, whereas embalming was a mythical labor aimed at immortalising a *hidden* dimension.

We need a visible past, a visible continuum, a visible myth of origin to reassure us as to our ends, since ultimately we have never believed in them. Whence that historic scene of the mummy's reception at Orly airport. All because Rameses was a great despot and military figure? Certainly: but above all because the order which our culture dreams of, behind that defunct power it seeks to annex, could have had nothing to do with it, and it dreams thus because it has exterminated this order by exhuming it *as if it were our own past*.

We are fascinated by Rameses as Renaissance Christians were by the American Indians: those (human?) beings who had never known the word of Christ. Thus, at the beginning of colonisation, there was a moment of stupor and amazement before the very possibility of escaping the universal law of the Gospel. There were two possible responses: either to admit that this law was not universal, or to exterminate the Indians so as to remove the evidence. In general, it was enough to convert them, or even simply to discover them, to ensure their slow extermination.

Thus it would have been enough to exhume Rameses to ensure his extermination by museumification. For mummies do not decay because of worms: they die from being transplanted from a prolonged symbolic order, which is master over death and putrescence, on to an order of history, science and museums—our own, which is no longer master over anything, since it only knows how to condemn its predecessors to death and putrescence and their subsequent resuscitation by science. An irreparable violence towards all secrets, the violence of a civilisation without secrets. The hatred by an entire civilisation for its own foundations.

And just as with ethnology playing at surrendering its object the better to establish itself in its pure form, so museumification is only one more turn in the spiral of artificiality. Witness the cloister of St-Michel de Cuxa, which is going to be repatriated at great expense from the Cloisters in New York to be reinstalled on "its original site". And everyone is supposed to applaud this restitution (as with the "experimental campaign to win back the sidewalks" on the Champs-Elysees!). However, if the exportation of the cornices was in effect an arbitrary act, and if the Cloisters of New

Jean Baudrillard

York are really an artificial mosaic of all cultures (according to a logic of the capitalist centralisation of value), then reimportation to the original location is even more artificial: it is a total simulacrum that links up with "reality" by a complete circumvolution.

The cloister should have stayed in New York in its simulated environment, which at least would have fooled no one. Repatriation is only a supplementary subterfuge, in order to make out as though nothing had happened and to indulge in a retrospective hallucination.

In the same way Americans flatter themselves they brought the number of Indians back to what it was before their conquest. Everything is obliterated only to begin again. They even flatter themselves they went one better, by surpassing the original figure. This is presented as proof of the superiority of civilisation: it produces more Indians than they were capable of themselves. By a sinister mockery, this overproduction is yet again a way of destroying them: for Indian culture, like all tribal culture, rests on the limitation of the group and prohibiting any of its "unrestricted" growth, as can be seen in the case of Ishi. Demographic "promotion", threfore, is just one more step towards symbolic extermination.

We too live in a universe everywhere strangely similar to the original—here things are duplicated by their own scenario. But this double does not mean, as in folklore, the imminence of death—they are already purged of death, and are even better than in life; more smiling, more authentic, in light of their model, like the faces in funeral parlors.

Hyperreal and Imaginary

Disneyland is a perfect model of all the entangled orders of simulation. To begin with it is a play of illusions and phantasms: Pirates, the Frontier, Future World, etc. This imaginary world is supposed to be what makes the operation successful. But what draws the crowds is undoubtedly much more the social microcosm, the miniaturised and *religious* revelling in real America, in its delights and drawbacks. You park outside, queue up inside, and are totally abandoned at the exit. In this imaginary world the only phantasmagoria is in the inherent warmth and affection of the crowd, and in that sufficiently excessive number of gadgets used there to specifically maintain the multitudinous affect. The contrast with the absolute solitude of the parking lot—a veritable concentration camp—is total. Or rather: inside, a whole range of gadgets magnetise the crowd into direct flows—outside, solitude is directed onto a single gadget: the automobile. By an extraordinary coincidence (one that undoubtedly belongs to the peculiar enchantment of this universe), this deep-frozen infantile world happens to have been conceived and realised by a man who is himself now cryogenised: Walt Disney, who awaits his resurrection at minus 180 degrees centigrade.

The objective profile of America, then, may be traced throughout Disneyland, even down to the morphology of individuals and the crowd. All its values are exalted here, in miniature and comic strip form. Embalmed and pacified. Whence the possibility of an ideological analysis of Disneyland (L. Marin does it well in *Utopies, jeux d'espaces*): digest of the American way of life, panegyric to American values, idealised transposition of a contradictory reality. To be sure. But this conceals something else, and that "ideological" blanket exactly serves to cover over a *third-order simulation*: Disneyland is there to conceal the fact that it is the "real" country, all of "real" America, which *is* Disneyland (just as prisons are there to conceal the fact that it is the social in its entirety, in its banal omnipresence, which is carceral). Disneyland is presented as imaginary in order to make us believe that the rest is real, when in fact all of Los Angeles and the America surrounding it are no longer real, but of the order of the hyperreal and of simulation. It is no longer a question of a false representation of reality (ideology), but of concealing the fact that the real is no longer real, and thus of saving the reality principle.

The Disneyland imaginary is neither true nor false; it is a deterrence machine set up in order to rejuvenate in reverse the fiction of the real. Whence the debility, the infantile degeneration of this imaginary. It is meant to be an infantile world, in order to make us believe that the adults are elsewhere, in the "real" world, and to conceal the fact that real childishness is everywhere, particularly amongst those adults who go there to act the child in order to foster illusions as to their real childishness.

Moreover, Disneyland is not the only one. Enchanted Village, Magic Mountain, Marine World: Los Angeles is encircled by these "imaginary stations" which feed reality, reality-energy, to a town whose mystery is precisely that it is nothing more than a network of endless, unreal circulation—a town of fabulous proportions, but without space or dimensions. As much as electrical and nuclear power stations, as much as film studios, this town, which is nothing more than an immense script and a perpetual motion picture, needs this old imaginary made up of childhood signals and faked phantasms for its sympathetic nervous system.

Political Incantation

Watergate. Same scenario as Disneyland (an imaginary effect concealing that reality no more exists outside than inside the bounds of the artificial perimeter): though here it is a scandal effect concealing that there is no difference between the facts and

26

their denunciation (identical methods are employed by the CIA and the *Washington Post* journalists). Same operation, though this time tending towards scandal as a means to regenerate a moral and political principle, towards the imaginary as a means to regenerate a reality principle in distress.

The denunciation of scandal always pays homage to the law. And Watergate above all succeeded in imposing the idea that Watergate *was* a scandal—in this sense it was an extraordinary operation of intoxication. The reinjection of a large dose of political morality on a global scale. It could be said along with Bourdieu that: "The specific character of every relation of force is to dissimulate itself as such, and to acquire all its force only because it is so dissimulated", understood as follows: capital, which is immoral and unscrupulous, can only function behind a moral superstructure, and whoever regenerates this public morality (by indignation, denunciation, etc.) spontaneously furthers the order of capital, as did the *Washington Post* journalists.

But this is still only the formula of ideology, and when Bourdieu enunciates it, he takes "relation of force" to mean the *truth* of capitalist domination, and he *denounces* this relation of force as itself a *scandal*—he therefore occupies the same deterministic and moralistic position as the *Washington Post* jounalists. He does the same job of purging and reviving moral order, an order of truth wherein the genuine symbolic violence of the social order is engendered, well beyond all relations of force, which are only its indifferent and shifting configuration in the moral and political consciousness of men.

All that capital asks of us is to receive it as rational or to combat it in the name of rationality, to receive it as moral or to combat it in the name of morality. For they are *identical*, meaning *they can be read another way*: before, the task was to dissimulate scandal; today, the task is to conceal the fact that there is none.

Watergate is not a scandal: this is what must be said at all cost, for this is what everyone is concerned to conceal, this dissimulation masking a strengthening of morality, a moral panic as we approach the primal (mise en) scene of capital: its instantaneous cruelty, its incomprehensible ferocity, its fundamental immorality—this is what is scandalous, unaccountable for in that system of moral and economic equivalence which remains the axiom of leftist thought, from Enlightenment theory to communism. Capital doesn't give a damn about the idea of the contract which is imputed to it—it is a monstrous unprincipled undertaking, nothing more. Rather, it is "enlightened" thought which seeks to control capital by imposing rules on it. And all that recrimination which replaced revolutionary thought today comes down to reproaching capital for not following the rules of the game. "Power is unjust, its justice is a class justice, capital exploits us, etc."—as if capital were linked by a contract to the society it rules. It is the left which holds out the mirror of equivalence, hoping that capital will fall for this phantasmagoria of the social contract and fulfull its obligation towards the whole of society (at the same time, no need for revolution: it is enough that capital accept the rational formula of exchange).

Capital in fact has never beeen linked by a contract to the society it dominates. It is a sorcery of the social relation, it is a *challenge to society* and should be responded to as such. It is not a scandal to be denounced according to moral and economic rationality, but a challenge to take up according to symbolic law.

Moebius-Spiralling Negativity

Hence Watergate was only a trap set by the system to catch its adversaries—a simulation of scandal to regenerative ends. This is embodied by the character called "Deep Throat", who was said to be a Republican grey eminence manipulating the leftist journalists in order to get rid of Nixon—and why not? All hypotheses are possible, although this one is superfluous: the work of the Right is done very well, and spontaneously, by the Left on its own. Besides, it would be naive to see an embittered good conscience at work here. For the Right itself also spontaneously does the work of the Left. All the hypotheses of manipulation are reversible in an endless whirligig. For manipulation is a floating causality where positivity and negativity engender and overlap with one another, where there is no longer any active or passive. It is by putting an *arbitrary* stop to this revolving causality that a principle of political reality can be saved. It is by the *simulation* of a conventional, restricted perspective field, where the premises and consequences of any act or event are calculable, that a political credibility can be maintained (including, of course, "objective" analysis, struggle, etc.). But if the entire cycle of any act or event is envisaged in a system where linear continuity and dialectical polarity no longer exist, in a field *unhinged by simulation*, then all determination evaporates, every act terminates at the end of the cycle having benefited everyone and been scattered in all directions.

Is any given bombing in Italy the work of leftist extremists, or of extreme right-wing provocation, or staged by centrists to bring every terrorist extreme into disrepute and to shore up its own failing power, or again, is it a police-inspired scenario in order to appeal to public security? All this is equally true, and the search for proof, indeed the objectivity of the fact does not check this vertigo of interpretation. We are in a logic of simulation which has nothing to do with a logic of facts and an order of reasons. Simulation is characterised by a *precession of the model*, of all models around the merest fact—the models come first, and their orbital (like the bomb) circulation constitutes the genuine magnetic field of events. Facts no longer have any trajectory of their own, they arise at the intersection of the models; a single fact may even be engendered by all the models at once. This anticipation, this precession, this short-circuit, this confusion of the fact with its model (no more divergence of meaning, no more dialectical polarity, no more negative electricity or implosion of poles) is what each time allows for all the possible interpretations, even the most contradictory—all are true, in the sense that their truth is exchangeable, in the image of the models from which they proceed, in a generalised cycle.

The communists attack the socialist party as though they wanted to shatter the Union of the Left. They sanction the idea that their reticence stems from a more radical political exigency. In fact, it is because they don't want power. But do they not want it at this conjuncture because it is unfavorable for the Left in general, or because it is unfavorable for them within the Union of the Left—or do they not want it by definition? When Berlinguer declares: "We musn't be frightened of seeing the communists seize power in Italy", this means simultaneously:

—that there is nothing to fear, since the communists, if they come to power, will change nothing in its fundamental capitalist mechanism,

—that there isn't any risk of their ever coming to power (for the reason that they don't want to)—and even if they did take it up, they will only ever wield it by proxy,

—that in fact power, genuine power, no longer exists, and hence there is no risk of anybody seizing it or taking it over,

—but more: I, Berlinguer, am not frightened of seeing the communists seize power in Italy—which might appear evident, but not that much, since

—this can also mean the contrary (no need of psychoanalysis here): *I am frightened* of seeing the communists seize power (and with good reason, even for a communist).

All the above is simultaneously true.

This is the secret of a discourse that is no longer only ambiguous, as political discourses can be, but that conveys the impossibility of a determinate position of power, the impossibility of a determinate position of discourse. And this logic belongs to neither party. It traverses all discourses without their wanting it.

Who will unravel this imbroglio? The Gordian knot can at least be cut. As for the Moebius strip, if it is split in two, it results in an additional spiral without there being any possibility of resolving its surfaces (here the reversible continuity of hypotheses). Hades of simulation, which is no longer one of torture, but of the subtle, maleficent, elusive twisting of meaning [4]—where even those condemned at Burgos are still a gift from Franco to Western democracy, which finds in them the occasion to regenerate its own flagging humanism, and whose indignant protestation consolidates in return Franco's regime by uniting the Spanish masses against foreign intervention? Where is the truth in all that, when such collusions admirably knit together without their authors even knowing it?

The conjunction of the system and its extreme alternative like two ends of a curved mirror, the "vicious" curvature of a political space henceforth magnetised, circularised, reversibilised from right ot left, a torsion that is like the evil demon of commutation, the whole system, the infinity of capital folded back over its own surface: transfinite? And isn't it the same with desire and libidinal space? The conjunction of desire and value, of desire and capital. The conjunction of desire and the law—the ultimate joy and metamorphosis of the law (which is why it is so well received at the moment): only capital takes pleasure, Lyotard said, before coming to think that *we* take pleasure in capital. Overwhelming versatility of desire in Deleuze, an enigmatic reversal which brings this desire that is "revolutionary by itself, and as if involuntarily, in wanting what it wants", to want its own repression and to invest paranoid and fascist systems? A malign torsion which reduces this revolution of desire to the same fundamental ambiguity as the other, historical revolution.

All the referentials intermingle their discourses in a circular, Moebian compulsion.

Not so long ago sex and work were savagely opposed terms: today both are dissolved into the same type of demand. Formerly the discourse on history took its force from opposing itself to the one on nature, the discourse on desire to the one on power—today they exchange their signifiers and their scenarios.

It would take too long to run through the whole range of operational negativity, of all those scenarios of deterrence which, like Watergate, try to regenerate a moribund principle by simulated scandal, phantasm, murder—a sort of hormonal treatment by negativity and crisis. It is always a question of proving the real by the imaginary, proving truth by scandal, proving the law by transgression, proving work by the strike, proving the system by crisis and capital by revolution, as for that matter proving ethnology by the dispossession of its object (the Tasaday)—without counting:

—proving theatre by anti-theatre
—proving art by anti-art
—proving pedagogy by anti-pedagogy
—proving psychiatry by anti-psychiatry, etc., etc.

Everything is metamorphosed into its inverse in order to be perpetuated in its purged form. Every form of power, every situation speaks of itself by denial, in order to attempt to escape, by simulation of death, its real agony. Power can stage its own murder to rediscover a glimmer of existence and legitimacy. Thus with the American presidents: the Kennedys are murdered because they still have a political dimension. Others— Johnson, Nixon, Ford—only had a right to puppet attempts, to simulated murders. But they nevertheless needed that aura of an artificial menace to conceal thay they were nothing other than mannequins of power. In olden days the king (also the god) had to die— that was his strength. Today he does his miserable utmost to pretend to die, so as to preserve the *blessing* of power. But even this is gone.

To seek new blood in its own death, to renew the cycle by the mirror of crisis, negativity and anti-power: this is the only alibi of every power, of every institution attempting to break the vicious circle of its irresponsibility and its fundamental non-existence, of its deja-vu and its deja-mort.

Jean Baudrillard

Strategy of the Real

Of the same order as the impossibility of rediscovering an absolute level of the real, is the impossibility of staging an illusion. Illusion is no longer possible, because the real is no longer possible. It is the whole *political* problem of the parody, of hypersimulation or offensive simulation, which is posed here.

For example: it would be interesting to see whether the repressive apparatus would not react more violently to a simulated hold-up than to a real one? For the latter only upsets the order of things, the right of property, whereas the other interferes with the very principle of reality. Transgression and violence are less serious, for they only contest the *distribution* of the real. Simulation is infinitely more dangerous, however, since it always suggests, over and above its object, that *law and order themselves might really be nothing more than a simulation.*

But the difficulty is in proportion to the peril. How to feign a violation and put it to the test? Go and simulate a theft in a large department store: how do you convince the security guards that it is a simulated theft? There is no "objective" difference: the same gestures and the same signs exist as for a real theft; in fact the signs incline neither to one side nor the other. As far as the established order is concerned, they are always of the order of the real.

Go and organise a fake hold-up. Be sure to check that your weapons are harmless, and take the most trustworthy hostage, so that no life is in danger (otherwise you risk committing an offence). Demand ransom, and arrange it so that the operation creates the greatest commotion possible—in brief, stay close to the "truth", so as to test the reaction of the apparatus to a perfect simulation. But you won't succeed: the web of artificial signs will be inextricably mixed up with real elements (a police officer will really shoot on sight; a bank customer will faint and die of a heart attack; they will really turn the phoney ransom over to you)—in brief, you will unwittingly find yourself immediately in the real, one of whose functions is precisely to devour every attempt at simulation, to reduce everything to some reality—that's exactly how the established order is, well before institutions and justice come into play.

In this impossibility of isolating the process of simulation must be seen the whole thrust of an order that can only see and understand in terms of some reality, because it can function nowhere else. The simulation of an offence, if it is patent, will either be punished more lightly (because it has no "consequences") or be punished as an offence to public office (for example, if one triggered off a police operation "for nothing")—but *never as simulation*, since it is precisely as such that no equivalence with the real is possible, and hence no repression either. The challenge of simulation is irreceivable by power. How can you punish the simulation of virtue? Yet as such it is as serious as the simulation of crime. Parody makes obedience and transgression equivalent, and that is the most serious crime, since it *cancels out the difference upon which the law is based*. The established order can do nothing against it, for the law is a second-order simulacrum whereas simulation is third-order, beyond true and false, beyond equivalences, beyond the rational distinctions upon which function all power and the entire social. Hence, *failing the real*, it is here that we must aim at order.

This is why order always opts for the real. In a state of uncertainty, it always prefers this assumption (thus in the army they would rather take the simulator as a true madman). But this becomes more and more difficult, for it is practically impossible to isolate the process of simulation, through the force of inertia of the real which surrounds us, the inverse is also true (and this very reversibility forms part of the apparatus of simulation and of power's impotency): namely, *it is now impossible to isolate the process of the real*, or to prove the real.

Thus all hold-ups, hijacks and the like are now as it were simulation hold-ups, in the sense that they are inscribed in advance in the decoding and orchestration rituals of the media, anticipated in their mode of presentation and possible consequences. In brief, where they function as a set of signs dedicated exclusively to their recurrence as signs, and no longer to their "real" goal at all. But this does not make them inoffensive. On the contrary, it is as hyperreal events, no longer having any particular contents or aims, but indefinitely refracted by each other (for that matter like so-called historical events: strikes, demonstrations, crises, etc. [5]), that they are precisely unverifiable by an order which can only exert itself on the real and the rational, on ends and means: a referential order which can only dominate referentials, a determinate power which can only dominate a determined world, but which can do nothing about that indefinite recurrence of simulation, about that weightless nebula no longer obeying the law of gravitation of the real—power itself eventually breaking apart in this space and becoming a simulation of power (disconnected from its aims and objectives, and dedicated to *power effects* and mass simulation).

The only weapon of power, its only strategy against this defection, is to reinject realness and referentiality everywhere, in order to convince us of the reality of the social, of the gravity of the economy and the finalities of production. For that purpose it prefers the discourse of crisis, but also—why not?—the discourse of desire. "Take your desires for reality!" can be understood as the ultimate slogan of power, for in a non-referential world even the confusion of the reality principle with the desire principle is less dangerous than contagious hyperreality. One remains among principles, and there power is always right.

Hyperreality and simulation are deterrents of every principle and of every objective; they turn against power this deterrence which is so well utilised for a long time itself. For, finally, it was capital which was the first to feed throughout its history on the destruction of every referential, of every human goal, which shattered every ideal distinction between true and false, good and evil, in order to establish a radical law of equivalence and exchange, the iron law of its power. It was the first to practice deterrence, abstraction, disconnection, deterritorialisation, etc.; and if it was capital which fostered reality, the reality principle, it was also the first to liquidate it in the extermination of every use value, of every real equivalence, of production and wealth, in the very sensation we have of the unreality of the stakes and the omnipotence of manipulation. Now, it is this very logic which is today hardened even more *against* it. And when it wants to fight this catastrophic spiral by secreting one last glimmer of reality, on which to found one last glimmer of power, it only multiplies the *signs* and accelerates the play of simulation.

As long as it was historically threatened by the real, power risked deterrence and simulation, disintegrating every contradiction by means of the production of equivalent signs. When it is threatened today by simulation (the threat of vanishing in the play of signs), power risks the real, risks crisis, it gambles on remanufacturing artificial, social, economic, political stakes. This is a question of life or death for it. But it is too late.

Whence the characteristic hysteria of our time: the hysteria of production and reproduction of the real. The other production, that of goods and commodities, that of *la belle epoque* of political economy, no longer makes any sense of its own, and has not for some time. What society seeks through production, and overproduction, is the restoration of the real which escapes it. That is why *contemporary "material" production is itself hyperreal*. It retains all the features, the whole discourse of traditional production, but it is nothing more than its scaled-down refraction (thus the hyperrealists fasten in a striking resemblance a real from which has fled all meaning and charm, all the profundity and energy of representation). Thus the hyper-realism of simulation is expressed every-where by the real's striking resemblance to itself.

Power, too, for some time now produces nothing but signs of its resemblance. And at the same time, another figure of power comes into play: that of a collective demand for *signs* of power—a holy union which forms around the disappearance of power. Every-body belongs to it more or less in fear of the collapse of the political. And in the end the game of power comes down to nothing more than the *critical* obsession with power—an obsession with its death, an obsession with its survival, the greater the more it disappears. When it has totally disappeared, logically we will be under the total spell of power—a haunting memory already fore-shadowed everywhere, manifesting at one and the same time the compulsion to get rid of it (nobody wants it any more, everbody unloads it on others) and the apprehensive pining over its loss. Melancholy for societies without power: this has already given rise to facism, that overdose of a powerful referential in a society which cannot terminate its mourning.

But we are still in the same boat: none of our societies knows how to manage its mourning for the real, for power, for the *social itself*, which is implicated in this same breakdown. And it is by an artificial revitalisation of all this that we try to escape it. *Undoubtedly this will even end up in socialism.* By an unforeseen twist of events and an irony which no longer belongs to history, it is through the death of the social that socialism will emerge—as it is through the death of God that religions emerge. A twisted coming, a perverse event, an unintelligible reversion to the logic of reason. As is the fact that power is no longer present except to conceal that there is none. A simulation which can go on indefinitely, since—unlike "true" power which is, or was, a structure, a strategy, a relation of force, a stake—this is nothing but the object of a social *demand*, and hence subject to the law of supply and demand, rather than to violence and death. Completely expunged from the *political* dimension, it is dependent, like any other commodity, on production and mass consumption. Its spark has disappeared—only the fiction of a political universe is saved.

Likewise with work. The spark of production, the violence of its stake no longer exists. Everybody still produces, and more and more, but work has subtly become something else: a need (as Marx ideally envisaged it, but not at all in the same sense), the object of a social "demand," like leisure, to which it is equivalent in the general run of life's options. A demand exactly proportional to the loss of stake in the work process. [6] The same change in fortune as for power: the *scenario* of work is there to conceal the fact that the work-real, the production-real, has disappeared. And for that matter so has the strike-real too, which is no longer a stoppage of work, but its alternative pole in the ritual scansion of the social calendar. It is as if everyone has "occupied" their work place or work post, after declaring the strike, and resumed production, as is the custom in a "self-managed" job, in exactly the same terms as before, by declaring themselves (and virtually being) in a state of permanent strike.

This isn't a science-fiction dream: everywhere it is a question of a doubling of the work process. And of a double or locum for the strike process—strikes which are incorporated like obsolescence in objects, like crisis in production. Then there is no longer any strikes or work, but both simultaneously, that is to say something else entirely: a *wizardry of work*, a *trompe l'oeil*, a scenodrama (not to say melodrama) of production, collective dramaturgy upon the empty stage of the social.

It is no longer a question of the *ideology* of work—of the traditional ethic that obscures the "real" labour process and the "objective" process of exploitation—but of the scenario of work. Likewise, it is no longer a question of the ideology of power, but of the *scenario* of power. Ideology only corresponds to a betrayal of reality by signs; simulation corresponds to a short-circuit of reality and to its reduplication by signs. It is always the aim of ideological analysis to restore the objective process; it is always a false problem to want to restore the truth beneath the simulacrum.

This is ultimately why power is so in

accord with ideological discourses and discourses on ideology, for these are all discourses of *truth*—always good, even and especially if they are revolutionary, to counter the mortal blows of simulation.

The End of the Panopticon

It is again to this ideology of the lived experience, of exhumation, of the real in its fundamental banality, in its radical authenticity, that the American TV-verite experiment on the Loud family in 1971 refers: 7 months of uninterrupted shooting. 300 hours of direct non-stop broadcasting, without script or scenario, the odyssey of a family, its dramas, its joys, ups and downs— in brief, a "raw" historical document, and the "best thing ever on television, comparable, at the level of our daily existence, to the film of the lunar landing." Things are complicated by the fact that this family came apart during the shooting: a crisis flared up, the Louds went their separate ways, etc. Whence that insoluble controversy: was TV responsible? What would have happened *if TV hadn't been there.*

More interesting is the phantasm of filming the Louds *as if TV wasn't there*. The producer's trump card was to say: "They lived as if we weren't there". An absurd, paradoxical formula—neither true, nor false: but utopian. The "as if *we* weren't there" is equivalent to "as if *you* were there". It is this utopia, this paradox that fascinated 20 million viewers, much more than the "perverse" pleasure of prying. In this "truth" experiment, it is neither a question of secrecy nor of perversion, but of a kind of thrill of the real, or of an aesthetics of the hyperreal, a thrill of vertiginous and phony exactitude, a thrill of alienation and of magnification, of distortion in scale, of excessive transparency all at the same time. The joy in an excess of meaning, when the bar of the sign slips below the regular water line of meaning: the non-signifier is elevated by the camera angle. Here the real can be seen to have never existed (but "as if you were there"), without the distance which produces perspective space and our depth vision (but "more true than nature"). Joy in the microscopic simulation which transforms the real into the hyperreal. (This is also a little like what happens in porno, where fascination is more metaphysical than sexual.)

This family was in any case already somewhat hyperreal by its very selection: a typical, California-housed, 3-garage, 5-children, well-to-do professional upper middle class ideal American family with an ornamental housewife. In a way, it is this statistical perfection which dooms it to death. This ideal heroine of the American way of life is chosen, as in sacrificial rites, to be glorified and to die under the fiery glare of the studio lights, a modern fatum. For the heavenly fire no longer strikes depraved cities, it is rather the lens which cuts through ordinary reality like a laser, putting it to death. "The Louds: simply a family who agreed to deliver themselves into the hands of television, and to die from it", said the producer. So it is really a question of a sacrificial process, of a sacrificial spectacle offered to 20 million Americans. The liturgical drama of a mass society.

TV-verite. Admirable ambivalent terms: does it refer to the truth of this family, or to the truth of TV? In fact, it is TV which is the Loud's truth, it is it which is true, it is it which renders true. A truth which is no longer the reflexive truth of the mirror, nor the perspective truth of the panoptic system and of the gaze, but the manipulative truth of the test which probes and interrogates, of the laser which touches and then pierces, of computer cards which retain your punched-out sequences, of the genetic code which regulates your combinations, of cells which inform your sensory universe. It is to this kind of truth that the Loud family is subjected by the TV medium, and in this sense it really amounts to a death sentence (but is it still a question of truth?).

The end of the panoptic system. The eye of TV is no longer the source of an absolute gaze, and the ideal of control is no longer that of transparency. The latter still presupposes an objective space (that of the Renaissance) and the omnipotence of a despotic gaze. This is still, if not a system of confinement, at least a system of scrutiny. No longer subtle, but always in a position of exteriority, playing on the opposition between seeing and being seen, even if the focal point of the panopticon may be blind.

It is entirely different when with the

Louds "You no longer watch TV, TV watches you (live)," or again: "You no longer listen to *Pas de Panique, Pas de Panique* listens to you"—switching over from the panoptic apparatus of surveillance (of *Discipline and Punish*) to a system of deterrence, where the distinction between active and passive is abolished. No longer is there any imperative to submit to the model, or to the gaze. "YOU are the model!" "YOU are the majority!" Such is the slope of a hyperrealist sociality, where the real is confused with the model, as in the statistic operation, or with the medium, as in the Loud's operation. Such is the later stage of development of the social relation, our own, which is no longer one of persuasion (the classical age of propaganda, ideology, publicity, etc.) but one of dis- suasion or deterrence: "YOU are news, you are the social, the event is you, you are involved, you can use your voice, etc." A turnabout of affairs by which it becomes impossible to locate an instance of the model, of power, of the gaze, of the medium itself, since *you* are always already on the other side. No more subject, focal point, center or periphery: but pure flexion or circular inflection. No more violence or surveillance: only "information," secret virulence, chain reaction, slow implosion and simulacra of spaces where the real-effect again comes into play.

We are witnessing the end of perspective and panoptic space (which remains a moral hypothesis bound up with every classical analysis of the "objective" essence of power), and hence the *very abolition of the spectacular*. Television, in the case of the Louds for example, is no longer a spectacular medium. We are no longer in the society of spectacle which the situationists talked about, nor in the specific types of alienation and repression which this implied. The medium itself is no longer identifiable as such, and the merging of the medium and the message (McLuhan[7]) is the first great formula of this new age. There is no longer any medium in the literal sense: it is now intangible, diffuse and diffracted in the real, and it can no longer even be said that the latter is distorted by it.

Such immixture, such a viral, endemic, chronic, alarming presence of the medium, without our being able to isolate its effects—

spectralised, like those publicity holograms sculptured in empty space with laser beams, the event filtered by the medium—the dissolution of TV into life, the dissolution of life into TV—an indiscernible chemical solution: we are all Louds, doomed not to invasion, to pressure, to violence and to blackmail by the media and the models, but to their induction, to their infiltration, to their illegible violence.

But we must be careful of the negative twist discourse gives this: it is a question neither of an illness nor of a viral complaint. Rather, we must think of the media as if they were, in outer orbit, a sort of genetic code which controls the mutation of the real into the hyperreal, just as the other, micromolecular code controls the passage of the signal from a representative sphere of meaning to the genetic sphere of the programmed signal.

The whole traditional mode of causality is brought into question: the perspective, deterministic mode, the "active," critical mode, the analytical mode—the distinction between cause and effect, between active and passive, between subject and object, between ends and means. It is in this mode that it can be said: TV watches us, TV alienates us, TV manipulates us, TV informs us . . . Throughout all this one is dependent on the analytical conception whose vanishing point is the horizon between reality and meaning.

On the contrary, we must imagine TV on the DNA model, as an effect in which the opposing poles of determination vanish according to a nuclear contraction or retraction of the old polar schema which has always maintained a minimal distance between a cause and an effect, between the subject and an object: precisely, the meaning gap, the discrepancy, the difference, the smallest possible margin of error, irreductible under penalty of reabsorption in an aleatory and indeterminable process which discourse can no longer even account for, since it is itself a determinable order.

It is this gap which vanishes in the genetic coding process, where indeterminacy is less a product of molecular randomness than a product of the abolition, pure and simple, of the *relation*. In the process of molecular control, which "goes" from the DNA nucleus to the "substance" it "informs," there is no more traversing of an effect, of an energy, of a determination, of any message. "Order, signal, impulse, message": all these attempt to render the matter intelligible to us, but by analogy, retranscribing in terms of inscription, vector, decoding, a dimension of which we know nothing—it is no longer even a "dimension," or perhaps it is the fourth (that which is defined, however, in Einsteinian relativity, by the absorption of the distinct poles of space and time). In fact, this whole process only makes sense to us in the negative form. But nothing separates one pole from the other, the initial from the terminal: there is just a sort of contraction into each other, a fantastic telescoping, a collapsing of the two traditional poles into one another: an IMPLOSION—an absorption of the radiating model of causality, of the differential mode of determination, with its positive and negative electricity—an implosion of meaning. *This is where simulation begins.*

Everywhere, in whatever political, biological, psychological, media domain, where the distinction between poles can no longer be maintained, one enters into simulation, and hence into absolute manipulation—not passivity, but the *non-distinction of active and passive*. DNA realises this aleatory reduction at the level of the living substance. Television itself, in the example of the Louds, also attains this *indefinite* limit where the family *vis-a-vis* TV are no more or less active or passive than is a living substance *vis-a-vis* its molecular code. In both there is only a nebula indecipherable into its simple elements, indecipherable as to its truth.

Orbital and Nuclear

The nuclear is the apotheosis of simulation. Yet the balance of terror is nothing more than the spectacular slope of a system of deterrence that has crept from the *inside* into all the cracks of daily life. The nuclear cliff-hanger only seals the trivialised system of deterrence at the heart of the media, of the inconsequential violence that reigns throughout the world, of the aleatory contrivance of every choice which is made for us. The slightest details of our behaviour are ruled by neutralised, indifferent, equivalent signs, by zero-sum signs like those which regulate "game strategy" (but the genuine equation is elsewhere, and the unknown is precisely that variable of simulation which makes the atomic arsenal itself a hyperreal form, a simulacrum which dominates us all and reduces all "ground-level" events to mere ephemeral scenarios, transforming the only life left to us into survival, into a wager without takers—not even into a death policy: but into a policy devaluated in advance).

It isn't that the direct menace of atomic destruction paralyses our lives. It is rather that deterrence leukemises us. And this deterrence come from the very situation which *excludes the real atomic clash*—excludes it beforehand like the eventuality of the real in a system of signs. Everybody pretends to believe in the reality of this menace (one understands it from the military point of view, the whole seriousness of their exercise, and the discourse of their "strategy," is at stake): but there are precisely no strategic stakes at this level, and the whole originality of the situation lies in the improbability of destruction.

Deterrence excludes war—the anti-quated violence of expanding systems. Deterrence is the neutral, implosive violence of metastable or involving systems. There is no subject of deterrence any more, nor adversary, nor strategy—it is a planetary structure of the annihilation of stakes. Atomic war, like that of Troy, will not take place. The risk of nuclear atomisation only serves as a pretext, through the sophistication of arms—but this sophistication exceeds any possible objective to such an extent that it is itself a symptom of nonexistence—to the installation of a universal system of security, linkup, and control whose deterrent effect does not aim for atomic clash at all (the latter has never been a real possibility, except no doubt right at the beginning of the cold war, when the nuclear posture was confused with conventional war) but really the much larger probability of any real event, of anything which could disturb the general system and upset the balance. The balance of terror is the terror of balance.

Deterrence is not a strategy. It circulates and is exchanged between the nuclear protagonists exactly like international capital in that orbital zone of monetary speculation, whose flow is sufficient to control all global finance. Thus *kill money* (not referring to *real* killing, any more than floating capital refers to real production) circulating in nuclear orbit is sufficient to control all violence and potential conflict on the globe.

What stirs in the shadow of this posture, under the pretext of a maximal "objective" menace, and thanks to that nuclear sword of Damocles, is the perfection of the best system of control which has never existed. And the progressive satellisation of the whole planet by that hypermodel of security.

The same goes for *peaceful* nuclear installations. Pacification doesn't distinguish between the civil and the military: wherever irreversible apparatuses of control are elaborated, wherever the notion of security becomes absolute, wherever the *norm* of security replaces the former arsenal of laws and violence (including war), the system of deterrence grows, and around it grows an historical, social and political desert. A huge involution makes every conflict, every opposition, every act of defiance contract in proportion to this blackmail which inter-rupts, neutralises and freezes them. No mutiny, no history can unfurl any more according to its own logic since it risks annihilation. No strategy is even possible any more, and escalation is only a puerile game left to the military. The political stake is dead. Only simulacra of conflict and carefully circumscribed stakes remain.

The "space race" played exactly the same role as the nuclear race. This is why it was so easily able to take over from it in the '60's (Kennedy/Khrushchev), or to develop concurrently in a mode of "peaceful coexistence." For what is the ultimate function of the space race, of lunar conquest, of satellite launchings, if not the institution of a model of universal gravitation, of satellisation, whose perfect embryo is the lunar module: a programmed microcosm, where *nothing can be left to chance*? Trajectory, energy, computation, physiology, psychology, the environment— nothing can be left to contingency, this is the total universe of the norm—the Law no longer exists, it is the operational immanence of every detail which is law. A universe purged of every threat to the senses, in a state of asepsis and weightlessness—it is this very perfection which is fascinating. For the exaltation of the masses was not in response to the lunar landing or the voyage of man in space (this is rather the fulfillment of an earlier dream)—no, we are dumbfounded by the perfection of their planning and technical manipulation, by the immanent wonder of programmed development. Fascinated by the maximisation of norms and by the mastery of probability. Unbalanced by the model, as we are by death, but without fear or impulse. For if the law, with its aura of transgression, if order, with its aura of violence, still taps a perverse imaginary, then the norm fixes, hypnotises, dumbfounds, causing every imaginary to involve. We no longer fantasise about every minutia of a program. Its observance alone unbalances. The vertigo of a flawless world.

The same model of planned infallibility, of maximal security and deterrence, now governs the spread of the social. That is the true nuclear fallout: the meticulous operation of technology serves as a model for the meticulous operation of the social. Here, too, *nothing will be left to chance*; moreover, this is the essence of socialisation, which has been going on for some centuries but which has now entered into its accelerated phase, towards a limit people imagined would be explosive (revolution), but which currently results in an inverse, irreversible, *implosive* process: a generalised deterrence of every chance, of every accident, of every trans-versality, of every finality, of every contra-diction, rupture or complexity in a sociality illuminated by the norm and doomed to the transparency of detail radiated by data-collecting mechanisms. In fact, the spatial and nuclear models do not even have their own ends: neither has lunar exploration, nor military and strategic superiority. Their truth lies in their being models of simulation, vector models of a system of planetary control (where even the super-powers of this scenario are not free—the whole world is satellised). [8]

Reject the evidence: with satellistation, the one who is satellised is not whom you might think. By the orbital inscription of a space object, the planet earth becomes a satellite, the terrestrial principle of reality becomes excentric, hyperreal and insignifi-cant. By the orbital establishment of a system of control like peaceful coexistence, all terrestrial microsystems are satellised and lose their autonomy. All energy, all events are absorbed by this excentric gravitation, everything condenses and implodes on the micro-model of control alone (the orbital satellite), as conversely, in the other, biological dimension everything converges and implodes on the molecular micro-model of the genetic code. Between the two, caught between the nuclear and the genetic, in the simultaneous assumption of the two fundamental codes of deterrence, every principle of meaning is absorbed, every deployment of the real is impossible.

The simultaneity of two events in July 1975 illustrates this in a striking way: the linkup in space of the two American and Soviet super-satellites, apotheosis of peaceful existence—and the suppression by the Chinese of character writing and conversion to the Roman alphabet. This latter signifies the "orbital" establishment of an abstract and model system of signs, into whose orbit will be reabsorbed all those once remarkable and singular forms of style and writing. The satellisation of their tongue: this is the way the Chinese enter the system of peaceful coexistence, which is inscribed in their sky at the very same time by the docking of the two satellites. The orbital flight of the Big Two, the neutralisation and homogenisation of everybody else on earth.

Yet, despite this deterrence by the orbital authority—the nuclear code or molecular—events continue at ground level, mishaps are increasingly more numerous, despite the global process of contiguity and simultaneity of data. But, subtly, these events no longer make any sense; they are nothing more than a duplex effect of simulation at the summit. The best example must be the Vietnam war, since it was at the crossroads of a maximal historical or "revolutionary" stake and the installation of this deterrent authority. What sense did that war make, if not that its unfolding sealed the end of history in the culminating and decisive event of our age?

Why did such a difficult, long and arduous war vanish overnight as if by magic?

Why didn't the American defeat (the greatest reversal in its history) have any internal repercussions? If it had truly signified a setback in the planetary strategy of the USA, it should have necessarily disturbed the internal balance of the American political system. But no such thing happened.

Hence something else took place. Ultimately this war was only a crucial episode in a peaceful coexistence. It marked the advent of China to peaceful coexistence. The long sought-after securing and concretising of China's non-intervention, China's apprenticeship in a global *modus vivendi*, the passing from a strategy of world revolution to one of a sharing of forces and empires, the transition from a radical alternative to political alternation in a now almost settled system (normalisation of Peking-Washington relations): all this was the stake of the Vietnam war, and in that sense, the USA pulled out of Vietnam but they won the war.

And the war "spontaneously" came to an end when the objective had been attained. This is why it was de-escalated, demobilised so easily.

The effects of this same remolding are legible in the field. The war lasted as long as there remained unliquidated elements irreducible to a healthy politics and a discipline of power, even a communist one. When finally the war passed from the rersistance to the hands of regular Northern troops, it could stop: it had attained its objective. Thus the stake was a political relay. When the Vietnamese proved they were no longer bearers of an unpredictable subversion, it could be handed over to them. That this was communist order wasn't fundamentally serious: it had proved itself, it could be trusted. They are even more effective than capitalists in liquidating "primitive" pre-capitalist and antiquated structures.

Same scenario as in the Algerian war.

The other aspect of this war and of all wars since: behind the armed violence, the murderous antagonism between adversaries— which seems a matter of life and death, and which is played as such (otherwise you could never send out people to get smashed up in this kind of trouble), behind this simulacrum of a struggle to death and of ruthless global stakes, the two adversaries are fundamentally as one against that other, unnamed, never mentioned thing, whose objective outcome in war, with equal complicity between the two adversaries, is total liquidation. It is tribal, communal, pre-capitalist structures, every form of exchange, language and symbolic organisation which must be abolished. Their murder is the object of war—and in its immense spectacular contrivance of death, war is only the medium of this process of terrorist rationalisation by the social—the murder through which sociality can be founded, no matter what allegiance, communist or capitalist. The total complicity or division of labour between two adversaries (who can even make huge sacrifices to reach that) for the very purpose of remolding and domesticating social relations.

"The North Vietnamese were advised to countenance a scenario of the liquidation of the American presence through which, of course, honour must be preserved."

The scenario: the extremely heavy bombardment of Hanoi. The intolerable nature of this bombing should not conceal the fact that it was only a simulacrum to allow the Vietnamese to seem to countenance a compromise and Nixon to make the Americans swallow the retreat of their forces. The game was already won, nothing was objectively at stake but the credibility of the final montage.

Moralists about war, champions of war's exalted values should not be greatly upset: a war is not any the less heinous for being a mere simulacrum—the flesh suffers just the same, and the dead ex-combatants count as much there as in other wars. That objective is always amply accomplished, like that of the partitioning of territories and of disciplinary sociality. What no longer exists is the adversity of adversaries, the reality of antagonistic causes, the ideological serious-ness of war—also the reality of defeat or victory, war being a process whose triumph lies quite·beyond these appearances.

In any case, the pacification (or deter-rence) dominating us today is beyond war and peace, the simultaneous equivalence of peace and war. "War is peace," said Orwell. Here, also, the two differential poles implode into each other, or recycle one another—a simultaneity of contradictions that is both the parody and the end of all dialectic. Thus it is possible to miss the truth of a war: namely, that it was well over before reaching a conclusion, that at its very core, war was brought to an end, and that perhaps it never ever began. Many other such events (the oil crisis, etc.) *never began*, never existed, except that artificial mishaps—abstracts, ersatzes of troubles, catastrophes and crises intended to maintain a historical and psychological investment under hypnosis. All media and the official news service only exist to maintain the illusion of actuality—of the reality of the stakes, of the objectivity of the facts. All events are to be read in reverse, where one perceives (as with the communists "in power" in Italy, the posthumous, "nostalgic" rediscovery of gulags and Soviet dissidents like the almost contemporary rediscovery, by a moribund ethnology, of the lost "difference" of Savages) that all these things arrive too late, with an overdue history, a lagging spiral, that they have exhausted their meaning long in advance and only survive on an artificial effervescence of signs, that all these events follow on illogically from one another, with a total equanimity towards the greatest inconsistencies, with a profound indifference to their consequences (but this is because there are none any more: they burn out in their spectacular promotion)—thus the whole newsreel of "the present" gives the sinister impression of kitsch, retro and porno all at the same time—doubtless everyone knows this, and nobody really accepts it. The reality of simulation is unendurable—more cruel than Artaud's Theatre of Cruelty, which was still an attempt at a dramaturgy of life, the last flickering of an ideal of the body, blood and violence in a system already sweeping towards a reabsorption of all the stakes without a trace of blood. For us the trick has been played. All dramaturgy, and even all real writing of cruelty has disappeared. Simulation is master, and nostalgia, the phantasmal parodic rehabilitation of all lost referentials, alone remain. Everything still unfolds before us, in the cold light of deterrence (including Artaud, who is entitled like all the rest to his revival, to a second existence as the *referential* of cruelty).

This is why nuclear proliferation increases neither the chance of atomic clash nor of accident—save in the interval where "young" powers could be tempted to use them for non-deterrent or "real" purposes (like the Americans did on Hiroshima—but precisely they alone were entitled to this "use value" of the bomb, while all those who have since acquired it are deterred from using it by the very fact of its possession). Entry into the atomic club, so amusingly named, very rapidly removes (like syndicalisation for the working world) any inclination towards violent intervention. Responsibility, control, censorship, self-deterrence always increases faster than the forces or weapons at our disposal: this is the secret of the social order. Thus the very possibility of paralysing a whole country with the flick of a switch *makes* it impossible that electrical engineers will ever utilise this weapon: the entire myth of the revolutionary and total strike collapses at the very moment when the means to so are available—but alas, *exactly because* the means to do so are available. This is deterrence in a nutshell.

Therefore it is altogether likely that one day we shall see the nuclear powers exporting atomic reactors, weapons and bombs to every latitude. After control by threat will succeed the much more effective strategy of pacification by the bomb and by its possession. "Small" powers, hoping to buy their independent strike force, will only buy the virus of deterrence, of their own deterrence. The same goes for the atomic reactors we have already sent them: so many neutron bombs knocking out all historical virulence, all risk of explosion. In this sense, the nuclear system institutes a universally accelerated process of *implosion*, it conceals everything around it, it absorbs all living energy.

The nuclear system is both the culminating point of available energy and the maximisation of systems controlling all energy. Lockdown and control grow as fast as (and undoubtedly even faster than) liberating potentialities. This was already the aporia of modern revolutions. It is still the absolute paradox of the nuclear system. Energies freeze by their own fire power, they deter themselves. One can't really see what project, what power, what strategy, what subject could possibly be behind this enclosure, this vast saturation of a system by its own hereafter neutralised, unusable, unintelligible, non-explosive forces—except the possibility of *an explosion towards the center*, or an *implosion* where all these energies are abolished in a catastrophic process (in the literal sense, that is to say in the sense of a reversion of the whole cycle towards a minimal point, of a reversion of energies towards a minimal threshold).

Translated by Paul Foss
and Paul Patton

Notes

1. Cf. J. Baudrillard, *L'echange symbolique et la mort*, ("L'ordre des simulacres"), Paris, Gallimard, 1975.

2. And which is not susceptible to resolution in transference. It is the entanglement of these two discourses which makes psychoanalysis interminable.

3. Cf. M. Perniola, "Icones, Visions, Simulacres," *Traverses/10*, p. 39.

4. This does not necessarily result in a despair of meaning, but just as much in an improvisation of meaning, of nonsense, or of several simultaneous senses which cancel each other out.

5. The energy crisis, the ecological setting, by and large, are themselves a *disaster film*, in the same style (and of the same value) as those which currently do so well for Hollywood. It is pointless to laboriously interpret these films by their relationship with an

"objective" social crisis, or even with an "objective" phantasm of disaster. It is in the other direction that we must say it is *the social itself which*, in contemporary discourse, *is organised according to a script for a disaster film*. (Cf. Makarius, "La strategie de la catastrophe," *Traverses/10*, p. 15.

6. To this flagging investment in work corresponds a parallel declining investment in consumption. Goodbye to use value or prestige of the automobile, goodbye to the amorous discourse which made a clearcut distinction between the object of enjoyment and the object of work. Another discourse takes over, which is a *discourse of work on the object of consumption* aiming at an active, compelling, puritan reinvestment (use less gas, look to your security, speed is obsolete, etc.), to which automobile specifications pretend to be adapted: rediscovering a stake by transposition of the poles. Thus work becomes the object of a need, the car becomes the object of work—no better proof of the inability to distinguish the stakes. It is by the very swing of voting "rights" to electoral "duties" that the disinvestment of the political sphere is signaled.

7. The medium/message confusion, of course, is a correlative of the confusion between sender and receiver, thus sealing the disappearance of all the dual, polar structures which formed the discursive organisation of language, referring to the celebrated grid of functions in Jacobson, the organisation of all determinate articulation of meaning. "Circular" discourse must be taken literally: that is, it no longer goes from one point to the other but describes a circle

that *indistinctly* incorporates the positions of transmitter and receiver, henceforth unlocatable as such. Thus there is no longer any instance of power, any transmitting authority—power is something that circulates and whose source can no longer be located, a cycle in which the positions of dominator and the dominated interchange in an endless reversion which is also the end of power in its classical definition. The circularisation of power, knowledge and discourse brings every localisation of instances and poles to an end. Even in psychoanalytic interpretation, the "power" of the interpreter does not come from any external authority, but from the interpreted themselves. This changes everything, for we can always ask the traditional holders of power where they get their power from. Who made you Duke? The King. And who made the King? God. God alone does not reply. But to the question: who made the psychoanalyst? the analyst quite easily replies: You. Thus is expressed, by an inverse simulation, the passage from the "analysed" to the "analysand," from active to passive, which only goes to describe the swirling, mobile effect of the poles, its effect of circularity in which power is lost, is dissolved, is resolved into complete manipulation (this is no longer of the order of the directive authority and the gaze, but of the order of personal contact and commutation). See, also, the State/family circularity secured by the floating and metastatic regulation of images of the social and the private. (J. Donzelot, *The Policing of Families*)

From now on, it is impossible to ask the famous

question:

"From what position do you speak?"—

"How do you know?"—

"From where do you get the power?", without immediately getting the reply: "But it is *of* (from) you that I speak"—meaning, it is you who speaks, is is you who knows, power is you. A gigantic circonvolution, circumlocution of the spoken word, which amounts to irredeemable blackmail and irremovable deterrence of the subject supposed to speak, but left without a word to say, responseless, since to questions asked can come the inevitable reply: but *you are* the reply, or: your question is already an answer, etc.—the whole sophistical stranglehold of word-tapping, forced confession disguised as free expression, trapping the subject in his own questioning, the precession of the reply about the question (the whole violence of interpretation is there, and the violence of the conscious or unconscious self-management of "speech).

This simulacrum of inversion or involution of poles, this clever subterfuge which is the secret of the whole discourse of manipulation and hence, today, in every domain, the secret of all those new powers sweeping clean the stage of power, forging the assumption of all speech from which comes that fantastic silent majority characteristic of our times—all this undoubtedly began in the political sphere with the democratic simulacrum, that is to say with the substitution of the instance of the people for the instance of God as source of power, and the substitution of power as *representation* for power as *emanation*. An anti-Copernican revolution: no longer any transcendent instance nor any sun nor any luminous source of power and knowledge—everything comes from and returns to the people. It is this magnificent *recycling* that the universal simulacrum of manipulation, from the scenario of mass suffrage to present-day and ilusory opinion polls, begins to be installed.

8. Paradox: all bombs are clean—their only pollution is the system of control and security they radiate *when they are not detonated*.

The Orders of Simulacra

Three orders of appearance, parallel to the mutations of the law of value, have followed one another since the Renaissance:

—*Counterfeit* is the dominant scheme of the "classical" period, from the Renaissance to the industrial revolution;

—*Production* is the dominant scheme of the industrial era;

—*Simulation* is the reigning scheme of the current phase that is controlled by the code.

The first order of simulacrum is based on the natural law of value, that of the second order on the commercial law of value, that of the third order on the structural law of value.

The Stucco Angel

Counterfeit (and fashion at the same time) is born with the Renaissance, with the destructuring of the feudal order by the bourgeois order and the emergence of open competition on the level of the distinctive signs. There is no such thing as fashion in a society of cast and rank, since one is assigned a place irrevocably, and so class mobility is non-existent. An interdiction protects the signs and assures them a total clarity; each each sign then refers unequivocally to a status. Likewise no counterfeit is possible with the ceremony—unless as black magic and sacrilege, and it is thus that any confusion of signs is punished: as grave infraction of the order of things. If we are starting to dream again, today especially, of a world of sure signs, of a strong "symbolic order," make no mistake about it: this order has existed and it was that of a ferocious hierarchy, since transparency and cruelty for signs go together. In caste societies, feudal or archaic, *cruel* societies, the signs are limited in number, and are not widely diffused, each one functions with its full value as interdiction, each is a reciprocal obligation between castes, clans or persons. The signs therefore are anything but arbitrary. The arbitrary sign begins when, instead of linking two persons in an unbreakable reciprocity, the signifier starts referring back to the disenchanted universe of the signified, common denominator of the real world toward which no one has any obligation.

End of the *obliged* sign, reign of the emancipated sign, that all classes will partake equally of. Competitive democracy succeeds the endogomy of signs proper to statutory order. At the same time we pass, with the transfer of values/signs of prestige from one class to another, necessarily into *counterfeit*. For we have passed from a limited order of signs, which prohibits "free production," to a proliferation of signs according to demand. But the sign multiplied no longer resembles in the slightest the obliged sign of limited diffusion: it is its counterfeit, not by corruption of an "original", but by extension of a material whose very clarity depended on the restriction by which it was bound. No longer discriminating (it is no more than competitive), unburdened of all restraint, universally available, the modern sign still simulates necessity in taking itself as tied somehow to the world. The modern sign dreams of the signs of the past and would well appreciate finding again, in its reference to the real, an *obligation*: but what it finds again is only a *reason*: this referential reason, this real, this "natural" off which it is going to live. But this bond of designation is only the simulacrum of symbolic obligation: it produces neutral values only, that can be exchanged in an objective world. The sign here suffers the same destiny as work. The "free" worker is free only to produce equivalents—the "free and emancipated" sign is free only to produce the signs of equivalence.

It is therefore in the simulacrum of a "nature" that the modern sign finds its value. Problematic of the "natural," metaphysics of reality and appearance: that is the history of the bourgeoisie since the Renaissance, mirror of the bourgeois sign, mirror of the classical sign. And still today the nostalgia for a natural referent of the sign is still alive, in spite of the revolutions that have come to break up this configuration, including one in production, where the signs refer no longer to any nature, but only to the law of exchange, and come under the commercial law of value.

It is in the Renaissance that the false is born along with the natural. From the fake shirt in front to the use of the fork as artificial prosthesis, to the stucco interiors and the great baroque theatrical machinery. The entire classical era belongs *par excellence* to the theatre. Theatre is the form which takes over social life and all of architecture from the Renaissance on. It's there, in the prowesses of stucco and baroque art, that you read the methapysic of the counterfeit and the new ambitions of Renaissance man—those of a *worldly demiurge*, a transubstantiation of all of nature into a unique substance, theatrical like social life unified under the sign of bourgeois values, beyond all differences in blood, rank, or of caste. Stucco means democracy triumphant over all artificial signs, the apotheosis of theatre and fashion, and it betrays the new classes' infinite capabilities, its power to do anything once it has been able to break through the exclusiveness of signs. The way lies open to unheard-of combinations, to all the games, all the counterfeits—the Promethean verve of the bourgeoisie first plunged into the *imitation of nature* before throwing itself into *production*. In the churches and palaces stucco is wed to all forms, imitates everything—velvet curtains, wooden corniches, charnel swelling of the flesh. Stucco exorcizes the unlikely confusion of matter into a single new substance, a sort of general equivalent of all the others, and is prestigious theatrical ly because is itself a representative substance, a mirror of all the others.

But simulacra are not only a game played with signs; they imply social rapports and social power. Stucco can come off as the exhaltation of a rising science and technology; it is also connected to the baroque—which in turn is tied to the enterprise of the Counter Reformation and the hegemony over the political and mental world that the Jesuits—who were the first to act according to modern conceptions of power—attempted to establish.

There is a strict correlation between the mental obedience of the Jesuits (*"perinde ac cadaver"*) and the demiurgic ambition to exorcize the natural substance of a thing in order to substitute a synthetic one. Just like a man submitting his will to his organization, things take on the ideal functionality of the cadaver. All technology, all technocracy are incipiently there: the presumption of an ideal counterfeit of the world, expressed in the invention of a universal substance and of a universal amalgam of substances. Reunify the scattered world (after the Reformation) under the aegis of a homogenous doctrine, universalize the world under a single word (from New Spain to Japan: the Missions), constitute a political elite *of the state*, with an identically centralized strategy: these are the objectives of the Jesuits. In order to accomplish this, you need to create effective simulacra: the apparatus of the organization is one, but also is clerkly magnificence and the theatre (the great theatre of the cardinals and grey eminences). And training and education are other simulacra that aimed, for the first time ever in a systematic manner, at remodeling an ideal nature from a child. That architectural sauce of stucco and baroque is a great apparatus of the same kind. All of the above precedes the productivist rationality of capital, but everything testifies already—not in production, but in counterfeit to the same project of control and universal hegemony—to a social scheme

Jean Baudrillard

where the internal coherence of a system is already at work.

Once there lived in the Ardennes an old cook, to whom the molding of buildings out of cakes and the science of plastic patisserie had given the ambition to take up the creation of the world where God had left it, in its natural phase, so as to eliminate its organic spontaneity and substitute for it a single, unique and polymorphous matter: Reinforced Concrete: concrete furniture, chairs, drawers, concrete sewing machines, and outside in the courtyard, an entire orchestra, including violins, of concrete—all concrete! Concrete trees with real leaves printed into them, a hog made out of reinforced concrete, but with a real hog's skull inside, concrete sheep covered with real wool. Camille Renault had finally found the original substance, the paste from which different things can only be distinguished by "realistic" nuance: the hog's skull, leaves of the tree—but this was doubtless only a concession of the demiurge to his visitors ... for it was with an adorable smile that this 80-year-old god received visitors to his creation. He sought no argument with divine creation;

he was remaking it only to render it more intelligible. Nothing here of a Luciferan revolt, or a will-to-parody, or of a desire to espouse the cause of naive art. The Ardennes cook reigned simply over a unified mental substance (for concrete is a *mental* substance; it allows, just like a concept, phenomena to be organized and divided up at will). His project was not so far from that of the builders in stucco of baroque art, nor very different from the projection on the terrain of an urban community in the current great ensembles. The counterfeit is working, so far, only on substance and form, not yet on relations and structures. But it is aiming already, on this level, at the control of a pacified society, ground up into a synthetic, deathless substance: an indestructible artifact that will guarantee an eternity of power. Is it not man's miracle to have invented, with plastic, a non-degradable material, interrupting thus the cycle which, by corruption and death, turns all the earth's substances ceaselessly one into another? A substance out-of-the-cycle; even fire leaves an indestructible residue. There is something incredible about it, this simulacrum where you can see in a condensed form the ambition of a universal semiotic. This has nothing to do with the "progress" of technology or with a rational goal for science. It is a project of political and cultural hegemony, the fantasy of a closed mental substance—like those angels of baroque stucco whose extremities meet in a curved mirror.

The Automation of the Robot

A whole world separates these two artificial beings. One is a theatrical counterfeit, a mechanical and clock-like man; technique submits entirely to *analogy* and to the effect of semblance. The other is dominated by the technical principle; the machine overrides all, and with the machine *equivalence* comes too. The automaton plays the part of courtier and good company; it participates in the pre-Revolutionary French theatrical and social games. The robot, on the other hand, as his name indicates, is a worker: the theatre is over and done with, the reign of mechanical man commences. The automaton is the *analogy* of man and remains his interlocutor (they play chess together!). The machine is man's *equivalent* and annexes him to itself in the unity of its operational process. This is the difference between a simulacrum of the first order and one of the second.

We shouldn't make any mistakes on this matter for reasons of "figurative" resemblance between robot and automaton. The latter is an interrogation upon nature, the mystery of the existence or non-existence of the soul, the dilemma of appearance and being. It is like God: what's underneath it all, what's inside, what's in the back of it? Only the counterfeit men allow these problems to be posed. The entire metaphysics of man as protagonist of the *natural theatre* of the creation is incarnated in the automaton, before disappearing with the Revolution. And the automaton has no other destiny than to be ceaselessly compared to living man—so as to be more natural than him, of which he is the ideal figure. A perfect double for man, right up to the suppleness of his movements, the functioning of his organs and intelligence—right up to touching upon the anguish there would be in becoming

Jean Baudrillard

aware that there is no difference, that the soul is over with and now it is an ideally naturalized body which absorbs its energy. Sacrilege. This difference is then always maintained, as in the case of that perfect automaton that the impersonator's jerky movements on stage imitate; so that at least, even if the roles were reversed, no confusion would be possible. In this way the interrogation of the automaton remains an open one, which makes it out to be a kind of mechanical optimist, even if the counterfeit always connotes something diabolical. [1]

No such thing with the robot. The robot no longer interrogates appearance; its only truth is in its mechanical efficacy. It is no longer turned towards a resemblance with man, to whom furthermore it no longer bears comparison. That infinitesimal metaphysical difference, which made all the charm and mystery of the automaton, no longer exists; the robot has absorbed it for its own benefit. Being and appearance are melted into a common substance of production and work. The first-order simulacrum never abolished difference. It supposes an always detectable alteration between semblance and reality (a particularly subtle game with trompe-l'oeil painting, but art lives entirely off of this gap). The second-order simulacrum simplifies the problem by the absorption of the appearances, or by the liquidation of the real, whichever. It establishes in any case a reality, image, echo, appearance; such is certainly work, the machine, the system of industrial production in its entirety, in that it is radically opposed to the principle of theatrical illusion. No more resemblance or lack of resemblance, of God, or human being, but an imminent logic of the operational principle.

From then on, men and machines can proliferate. It is even their law to do so—which the automatons never have done, being instead sublime and singular mechanisms. Men themselves only started their own proliferation when they achieved the status of machines, with the industrial revolution. Freed from all resemblance, freed even from their own double, they expand like the system of production, of which they are only the miniaturized equivalent. The revenge of the simulacrum that feeds the myth of the sorcerer's apprentice doesn't happen with the automaton. It is, on the other hand, the very law of the second type; and from that law proceeds still the hegemony of the robot, of the machine, and of dead work over living labor. This hegemony is necessary for the cycle of production and reproduction. It is with this reversal that we leave behind the counterfeit to enter (re)production. We leave natural law and the play of its forms to enter the realm of the mercantile law of value and its calculations of force.

The Industrial Simulacrum

It is a new generation of signs and objects which comes with the industrial revolution. Signs without the tradition of caste, ones that will never have known any binding restrictions. They will no longer have to be *counterfeited,* since they are going to be produced all at once on a gigantic scale. The problem of their uniqueness, or their origin, is no longer a matter of concern; their origin is technique, and the only sense they possess is in the dimension of the industrial simulacrum.

Which is to say the series, and even the possibility of two or of *n* identical objects. The relation between them is no longer that of an original to its counterfeit—neither analogy nor reflection—but equivalence, indifference. In a series, objects become undefined simulacra one of the other. And so, along with the objects, do the men that produce them. Only the obliteration of the original reference allows for the generalized law of equivalence, that is to say the *very possibility of production*.

The entire analysis of production changes according to whether you no longer see in it an original process, or even one that is at the core of all the others, but on the contrary a process of absorption of all original being and of introduction to a series of identical beings. Until now we have considered production and work as potential, as force, as historical process, as generic activity; the energetic-economic myth proper to modernity. We must now ask if production does not interfere *in the order of signs*, as a *particular* phase—if it is not basically only an episode in the line of simulacra: that precisely when, thanks to technique, potentially identical beings are produced in an indefinite series.

The immense energies that are at work in technique, industry, and the economy should not hide the fact that it is basically only a matter of attaining to that indefinite reproductibility. That is the challenge certainly to the "natural" order, but finally is only a second-order simulacrum, and rather inadequate as an imaginary solution to the problem of mastering the world. By comparison to the era of the counterfeit (the time of the double and the mirror, of theatre and the games of mask and appearance), the serial and technical era of reproduction is all-in-all a time of lesser scope (the era that follows—that of models of simulation and of third-order simulacra—is of more considerable dimension).

It is Walter Benjamin who, in *The Work of Art in the Era of its Technical Reproductibility*, first elicited the implications essential in this principle of reproduction. He shows that reproduction absorbs the process of production, changing its finalities and altering the status of product and producer. He demonstrates this mutation on the terrain of art, cinema and photography, because it is there that open up, in the 20th century, new territories without a tradition of classical productivity, and that are placed immediately under the sign of reproduction. But we know that today all material production enters into this sphere. We know that now it is on the level of reproduction (fashion, media, publicity, information and communication networks), on the level of what Marx negligently called the nonessential sectors of capital (we can hereby take stock of the irony of history), that is to say in the sphere of simulacra and of the code, that the global process of capital is founded. Benjamin first (and later McLuhan) understood technique not as a "productive force" (wherein marxist analysis is locked) but as medium, as form and principle of a whole new generation of sense. The fact alone that anything might be simply reproduced, as such, in two copies, is already a revolution; you only have to consider the shock of the African native seeing, for the very first time, two identical books. That these two products of technique should be *equivalent* under the sign of socially necessary work is less important in the long run than the *serial* repetition of the same object (which is also that of individuals as force-of-work). Technique as medium dominates not only the "message" of the product (it's use-value) but also the force-of-work that Marx wished to make the revolutionary message of production. Benjamin and McLuhan saw this matter more clearly than Marx; they saw the true message: *the true ultimatum was in reproduction itself.* And that production no longer has any sense; its social finality is lost in the series. The simulacra win out over history.

Furthermore, this stage of serial reproduction (that of the industrial mechanism, of the factory belt, of expanded reproduction) is ephemeral. As soon as dead work wins out over living work—that is, as soon as the era of primitive accumulation is over—serial production yields to generation by means of models. And here it is a question of a reversal of origin and finality, for all the forms change once they are not so much mechanically reproduced but even *conceived from the point-of-view of their very reproducibility*, diffracted from a generating nucleus we call the model. Here we are in the third-order simulacra; no longer that of the counterfeit of an original as in the first-order, nor that of the pure series as in the second. Here are the models from which proceed all forms according to the modulation of their differences. Only affiliation to the model makes sense, and nothing flows any longer according to its end, but proceeds from the model, the "signifier of reference," which is a kind of anterior finality and the only resemblance there is. We are in simulation in the modern sense of the word, of which industrialization is but the final manifestation. Finally, it is not serial reproductibility which is fundamental, but the modulation. Not quantitative equivalences, but distinctive oppositions. No longer the law of capital, but the structural law of value. And not only shouldn't we look to technique or the economy for the secrets of the code; it is, on the contrary, the very possibility of industrial production that we should look for in the genesis of the code and the simulacra. Each order submits to the order following. Just like the order of the counterfeit was abolished by that of serial production (we can see how art has passed entirely into the realm of the "mechanical"), so in the same way the entire order of production is in the process of tumbling into operational simulation.

The analyses of Benjamin and McLuhan are situated on these limits of reproduction and simulation, at the point where referential reason disappears, and where production is no longer sure of itself. In this sense they mark a decisive progress compared to the analyses of Veblen and Goblot. These latter, describing for example the signs of fashion, still refer to the classical configuration: the signs constitute a distinct material, have a finality and use for prestige, status, social differentiation. They manifest a strategy contemporaneous to that of profit and merchandise with Marx, at a time when you could still talk about the use-value of a sign or of force-of-work, when purely and simply, one could still talk about an economy because there was still a Reason of the sign, and a Reason of production.

The Metaphysic of the Code

> "Leibniz, that mathematical spirit, saw in the mystic elegance of the binary system that counts only the zero and the one, the very image of creation. The unity of the supreme Being, operating by binary function in nothingness, would have sufficed to bring out of it all the beings."
> ——McLuhan

The great simulacra constructed by man pass from a universe of natural laws to a universe of force and tensions of force, today to a universe of structures and binary oppositions. After the metaphysic of being and appearance, after that of energy and determination, comes that of indeterminacy and the code. Cybernetic control, generation from model, differential modulation, feed-back, question/answer, etc.: such is the new *operational* configuration (industrial simulacra are only *operational*). Digitality is its metaphysical principle (the God of Leibniz), and DNA its prophet. It is in effect in the genetic code that the "genesis of simulacra" today finds its most accomplished form. At the limit of an always more extensive abolition of references and finalities, of the loss of resemblance and designation, we find the digital program-sign, whose value is purely tactical, at the intersection of the other signals (corpuscles of information/test) and whose structure is that of a macro-molecular code of command and control.

At this level the question of signs, of their rational destination, their real or imaginary, their repression, their deviation, the illusion they create or that which they conceal, or their parallel meanings—all of that is erased. We have already seen signs of the first order, complex signs and rich in illusion, change, with the machines, into crude signs, dull, industrial, repetitive, echoless, operational and efficacious. What a mutation, even more radical still, with signals of the code, illegible, with no gloss possible, buried like programmatic matrices light-years away in the depths of the "biological" body—black boxes where all the commandments, all the answers ferment! End of the theatre of representation, the space of signs, their conflict, their silence; only the black box of the code, the molecular emitter of signals from which we have been irradiated, crossed by answers/questions like signifying radiations, tested continuously by our own program inscribed in the cells. Jail cells, electronic cells, party cells, microbiological cells: always the search for the smallest indivisible element, whose organic synthesis would be made according to the givens of the code. But the code itself is but a genetic cell, a generator where myriads of intersections produce all the questions and possible solutions, so that choices (by whom?) can be made. No finality involved with these "questions" (informational and signifying impulsions) but the answer, genetically unchangeable or inflected by minute and aleatory differences. Space is no longer even linear or one-dimensional: *cellular* space, indefinite generation of the same signals, like the tics of a prisoner gone crazy with solitude and repetition. Such is the genetic code: an erased record, unchangeable, of which we are no more than cells-for-reading. All aura of sign, of significance itself is resolved in this determination; all is resolved in the inscription and decodage.

Such is the third-order simulacrum, our

own. Such is the "mystic elegance of the binary system, of the zero and the one", from which all being proceeds. Such is the status of the sign that is also the end of signification: DNA or operational simulation.

All of this is perfectly well summed up by Sebeok ("Genetics and Semiotics", in *Versus*):

> Numerous observations confirm the hypothesis that the internal organic world descends in a straight line from the primordial forms of life. The most remarkable fact is the omnipresence of the DNA molecule. The genetic material of all organisms known on earth is in great measure made up of the nucleonic acids DNA and RNA that contain in their information structure, transmitted by reproduction from one generation to another and furthermore gifted with the capacity of self-reproduction and imitation. Briefly, the genetic code is universal, or almost. Its deciphering was an immense discovery, in the sense that it showed that "the two languages of the great polymers, the language of nucleonic acid and that of protein, are tightly correlated" (Crick, 1966; Clarck/Narcker, 1968); The Soviet mathematician Liapounov demonstrated in 1963 that all living systems transmit by prescribed canals with precision a small

quantity of energy or of matter containing a great volume of information, which is responsible for the ulterior control of a great quantity of energy and matter. In this perspective numerous phenomena, biological as well as cultural (stockage, feed-back, canalization of messages and others) can be seen as aspects of the treatment of information. In the last analysis information appears in great part as the repetition of information, or even as another sort of information, a sort of control that seems to be a universal property of terrestrial life, independent of form or substance.

Five years ago I drew attention to the convergence of genetics and linguistics— autonomous disciplines, but parallel in the larger field of communication science (of which animal semiotics alsi is a part). The terminology of genetics is full of expressions taken from linguistics and communication theory (Jacobson, 1968), which also underlined either the major resemblances or the important differences of structure and of function between genetic and verbal codes. . . It is obvious today that the genetic code must be considered the most fundamental of all the semiotic networks, and therefore a prototype of all the other systems of signaling that animals use, man included. From this point of view, molecules which are systems of quanta and behave like stable vehicles of physical information, systems of animal semiotics and cultural systems, including language, constitute a continuous chain of stages, with always more complex energy levels, in the framework of a universal unique evolution. It is therefore possible to describe either language or living systems from a unified cybernetic point-of-view. For the present, this is only a useful analogy or a prediction. A reciprocal rapprochement between animal communication and linguistics can lead to a complete knowledge of the dynamics of semiotics, and such a knowledge can be revealed, in the last analysis, to be nothing less than the very definition of life.

And so the current strategic model is designed that everywhere is replacing the great ideological model which constituted political economy in its time.

You will find it under the rigorour sign of "science" in the *Chance and Necessity* of Jacques Monod. The end of dialectical evolution, it is the discontinuous indeterminism of the genetic code that now controls life—the teleological principle. Finality no longer belongs to the term; there is no longer a term, nor a determination. Finality is there beforehand, inscribed in the code. We see that nothing has changed—simply the order of ends yields to the play of molecules, and the order of signifieds to the play of infinitesimal signifiers, reduced to their aleatory commutation. All the transcendant finalities reduced to a dashboard full of instruments. There is still, however, recourse to a nature, to an inscription in "biological" nature—in actuality, a nature distorted by fantasy like she always was, metaphysical sanctuary no longer of origin and substance, but this time of the code; the code must have an "objective" basis. What could be better for that purpose than the molecule and genetics? Monod is the strict theologian of this molecular transcendance, Edgar Morin the rapt disciple (A.D.N.* + Adonai!). But for one as well as the other, the fantasy of the code, which is equivalent to the reality of power, is merged with molecular idealism.

Thus we find once more in history that delirious illusion of unting the world under

*D.N.A.

the aegis of a single principle—that of a homogenous substance with the Jesuits of the Counter Reformation; that of the genetic code with the technocrats of biological science (but also linguistics as well), with Leibniz and his binary divinity as precursor. For the program here aimed at has nothing genetic about it, it is a social and historical program. That which is hypostatized in biochemistry is the ideal of a social order ruled by a sort of genetic code of macro-molecular calculation, of P.P.B.S. (Planned Programming Budgeting System), irradiating the social body with its operational circuits. The technical cybernetic finds its "natural philosophy" here, as Monod says. The fascination of the biological, of the biomedical dates from the very beginnings of science. It was at work in Spencerian organicism (sociobiology) on the level of second- and third-order structures (Jacob's classification in *The Logic of Life*, it is active today in modern biochemistry, on the level of structures of the fourth-order).

Coded similarities and dissimilarities: that is certainly the image of cyberniticized social exchange. You only have to add "stereospecific complex" in order to re-inject intracellular communication; that Morin will come to transfigure into molecular Eros.

Practically and historically, this signified the substitution of social control by the *end* (and by a more or less dialectical *providence* which surveys the accomplishment of this *end*) for social control by anticipation, simulation and programming, and indeterminate mutation directed by the code. Instead of a process which is finalized according to its ideal development, we generalize from a *model*. Instead of a right to a prophecy, we have the right of *registration*. There is no really radical difference between the two, only the schemes of control have become fantastically perfected. From a capitalist-productivist society to a neo-capitalist cybernetic order that aims now at total control. This is the mutation for which the biological theorization of the code prepares the ground. There is nothing of an accident in this mutation. It is the end of a history in which, successively, God, Man, Progress, and History itself die to profit the code, in which transcendance dies to profit immanence, the latter corresponding to a much more advanced phase in the vertiginous manipulation of social rapports.

In its indefinite reproduction, the system puts an end to the myth of its origin and to all the referential values it has itself secreted along the way. Putting an end to its myth of beginning, it ends its internal contradictions (no more real or referential to be confronted with), and it puts an end also to the myth of its own end: the revolution itself. What was profiled with revolution was the victory of human and generic reference, of the original potential of man. But if capital erases from the map generic man himself (for the sake of genetic man?) the Golden Age of the revolution was that of capital, where the myths of origin and end still circulated. Once short-circuited the myths (and the only danger capital confronted historically came to it from this *mythical* exigency of rationality that accompanied it from the very beginning) in an operationality of fact and without discourse, once capital itself has become its own myth, or rather an interminable machine, aleatory, something like a *social genetic code*, it no longer leaves any room for a planned reversal; and this is its true violence. It remains to be seen if this operationality is not itself a myth, if DNA is not also a *myth*.

Once and for all there is posed, in effect, the problem of science as discourse. A good occasion to pose it here, where this discourse is absolutized with such candor. "Plato, Heraclitus, Hegel, Marx: these ideological edifices, presented as *a priori*, were really *a posteriori* constructions, destined to justify a preconceived ethico-political theory . . . The only *a priori* for science is the postulate of objectivity, that forbids itself any part in this debate." (Monod). But this postulate results itself from a never innocent decision for objectification of the world and of the "real." In fact it is the coherence of a certain *discourse*, and all scientific movement is nothing but the space of this discourse, never revealing itself as such, and the "objective" simulacrum of which hides the political, strategic word. A little farther on, furthermore, Monod very well expresses the arbitrary nature of this phenomenon: "We might wonder if all the invariance, conservations and symmetries that constitute the scheme of scientific discourse are only fictions substituted for reality so as to offer an operational image. . . A logic founded on a purely abstract principle of identity possibly conventional. Convention, however, that human reason seems incapable of doing without." You couldn't say it better: that science has selected itself as generating formula, a model discourse, upon the faith of a conventional order (not just any, however; that of total reduction). But Monod slides rapidly into this dangerous hypothesis of a "conventional" identity principle. It would be better to base science, more crudely, upon an "objective" reality. Physics is there to witness that identity is only a postulate—it is *within things*, since there is "absolute identity of two atoms in the same quantitative state." Well then? Convention, or objective reality? The truth is that science is organized, like any other discourse, on the basis of a conventional logic, but it demands for its justification, like any other ideological discourse, a real "objective" reference, in a process of substance. If the principle of identity is somehow "true," even at the infinitesimal level of two atoms, then the entire conventional edifice of science that derives its inspiration from that level is also "true." The hypothesis of the genetic code, DNA, is also true and unsurpassable. So it goes with metaphysics.

Science accounts for things previously encircled and formalized so as to be sure to obey it. "Objectivity" is nothing else than that, and the ethic which comes to sanction this objective knowlegde is nothing less than a system of defense and imposed ignorance, whose goal is to preserve this vicious circle intact. [2]

"Down with all hypotheses that have allowed the belief in a true world," said Nietzsche.

The Tactile and the Digital

This regulation on the model of the genetic code is not at all limited to laboratory effects or to the exalted visions of theoreticians. Banal, everyday life is invested by these models. Digitality is with us. It is that which haunts all the messages, all the signs of our societies. The most concrete form you see it in is that of the test, of the question/answer, of the stimulus/response. All content is neutralized by a continual procedure of directed interrogation, of verdicts and ultimatums to decode, which no longer arise this time from the depths of the genetic code but that have the same tactical indeterminacy—the cycle of sense

being infinitely shortened into that of question/
answer, of bit or minute quantity of energy/
information coming back to its beginning, the
cycle only describing the perpetual reactualiza-
tion of the same models. The equivalent of the
total neutralization of the signified by the code
is the instantaneousness of the verdict of
fashion, or of any advertising or media
message. Any place where the offer swallows
up the demand, where the question assimilates
the answer, or absorbs and regurgitates it in a
decodable form, or invents and anticipates it in
a predictible form. Everywhere the same
"scenario," the scenario of "trial and error" (guinea
pigs in laboratory experiments), the scenario of
the breadth of choice offered everywhere ("the
personality test")—everywhere the test func-
ctions as a fundamental form of control, by
means of the infinite divisibility of practices and
responses.

We live by the mode of *referendum* precisely
because there is no longer any *referential*. Every
sign, every message (objects of "functional" use
as well as any item of fashion or televised news,
poll or electoral consultation) is presented to us
as question/answer. The entire system of
communication has passed from that of a

syntactically complex language structure to a binary sign system of question/answer—of perpetual *test*. Now tests and referenda are, we know, perfect forms of simulation: the answer is called forth by the question, it is design-ated in advance. *The referendum is always an ultimatum*: the unilateral nature of the question, that is no longer exactly an interrogation, but the immediate imposition of a sense whereby the cycle is suddenly completed. Every message is a verdict, just like the one that comes from polling statistics. The simulacrum of distance (or even of contradiction between the two poles) is only—like the effect of the real the sign seems to emit—a tactical hallucination.

Benjamin analyzes concretely, on the level of the technical instrument, this operation of the test:

> The performance of the movie actor is transmitted to the public by means of an array of technical instruments, with a twofold consequence. The camera that presents the performance of the film actor to the public need not respect the performance as an integral whole. Guided by the cameraman, the camera continually changes its position with respect to the performance. The sequence of positional views which the

editor composes from the material supplied him constitutes the completed film... Hence, the performance of the actor is subjected to a series of optical tests. This is the first consequence of the fact that the actor's performance is presented by means of the camera. Also, the film actor lacks the opportunity of the stage actor to adjust to the audience during the performance, since he does not present his performance to the audience in person. This permits the audience to take the position of the critic, without experiencing any personal contact with the actor. The audience's identification with the actor is really an identification with the camera. Consequently the audience takes the position of the camera; its approach is that of testing.

Note: The expansion of the field of the testable which mechanical equipment brings about for the actor corresponds to the extraordinary expansion of the field of the testable brought about for the individual through economic conditions. Thus, vocational aptitude tests become constantly more important. What matters in these tests are segmental performances of the individual. The film shot and the vocational aptitude test are taken before a committee of experts. The camera director in the studio occupies a place identical with that of the examiner during

aptitude tests. (Translated by H. Zohn in
Illuminations, from "The Work of Art in the
Age of Mechanical Reproduction.")

"The work of art with the dadaists
becomes a projectile. It plunges in on the
spectator, it takes on a tactile quality. The
diverging element in film is also first-and-
foremost a tactile element, based effectually
on the constant change of place and camera
angles that stimulate the spectator."

No contemplation is possible. The images
fragment perception into successive sequences,
into stimuli toward which there can be only
instantaneous response, yes or no—the limit of
an abbreviated reaction. Film no longer allows
you to question. It questions you, and directly. It
is in this sense that the modern media call for,
according to McLuhan, [3] a greater degree of
immediate participation, an incessant response,
a total plasticity (Benjamin compares the work
of the cameraman to that of the surgeon:
tactility and manipulation). The role of the
message is no longer information, but testing
and polling, and finally control ("contra-role," in
the sense that all your answers are already
inscribed in the "role," on the anticipated
registers of the code). Montage and codification

demand, in effect, that the receiver construe and decode by observing the same procedure whereby the work was assembled. The reading of the message is then only a perpetual examination of the code.

Every image, every media message, but also any functional environmental object, is a test—that is to say, in the full rigor of the term, liberating response mechanisms according to stereotypes and analytic models. Today, the object is no longer "functional" in the traditional meaning of the word; it no longer serves you, it *tests* you. It has nothing to do with the object of yesteryear, no more than does media news with a "reality" of facts. Both objects and information result already from a selection, a montage, from a point-of-view. They have already tested "reality," and have asked only questions that "answered back" to them. They have broken down reality into simple elements that they have reassembled into scenarios of regulated oppositions, exactly in the same way that the photographer imposes his contrasts, lights, angles on his subject (any photographer will tell you: you can do anything, all you have to do is approach the original from the right angle, at that right moment or mood that will render it the *correct answer* to the instantaneous test of the instrument and its code). It is exactly like the test or the referendum when they translate a conflict or problem into a game of question/answer. And reality, thus tested, tests you according to the same grill; you decode it according to the same code, inscribed within each message and object like a miniaturized genetic code.

All is presented today in a spread-out series, or as part of a line of products, and this fact alone tests you already, because you are obliged to make decisions. This approximates our general attitude toward the world around us to that of a *reading*, and to a selective deciphering. We live less like users than readers and selectors, reading cells. But nevertheless: by the same token you also are constantly selected and tested by the medium itself. Just like cutting out a sample for the ends of the survey, the media frame and excise their message bundles, which are in fact bundles of selected questions, samples of their audience. By a circular operation of experimental modification, of incessant interference, like a nervous input, tactile and retractile, that explores an object by means of brief perceptive sequences, until it has been localized and controlled. What the media thereby localize and control are no real and autonomous groups, but samples, samples modelled socially and mentally by a barrage of messages. "Public opinion" is evidently the prettiest of these samples—not an unreal political substance, but one that is hyperreal—a fantastic hyperreality that lives only off of montage and test-manipulation.

The eruption of the binary scheme question/answer is of an incalculable importance. It renders inarticulate every discourse. It short-circuits all that was, in a golden age come again, the dialectic of signifier and signified, of a representing and a represented. It is the end of objects whose meaning would be function, and of opinions that "representative" representatives would be able to vote for. It is the end of the real interrogation to which it was possible to answer (the end especially to unanswerable questions). This process has been entirely overthrown. The contradictory process of true and false, of real and the imaginary, is abolished in this hyperreal logic of ▼montage. Michel Tort, in his book *Intelligence Quotient*, analyzes this quite well: "What is going to determine the answer to the question is not the question as such in the form in which it was posed, it is also the idea that the interrogated subject forms about the most appropriate tactic to adopt in function of the concept he has formed about the expectations of the interrogator." And further: "The artifact is something else entirely than a controlled transformation of the object for the ends of knowledge: it is a rude interference with reality, at the end of which it is impossible to say what in reality can be objectively known and what is the result of technical intervention (medium). The I.Q. is an artifact." No more true or false, because no more distinguishable hiatus between question and response. In the light of the tests, intelligence, like opinion—and more generally the entire process of meaning—is reduced to the "ability to produce contrasting reactions to a growing series of adequate stimuli."

This entire analysis sends us back to McLuhan's formula: "The Medium is the Message." It is in effect the medium—the very style of montage, of decoupage, of interpella- tion, solicitation, summation, by the medium— which controls the process of meaning. And you understand why McLuhan saw in the era of the great electronic media an era of *tactile* communication. We are closer here in effect to the tactile than to the visual universe, where the distancing is greater and reflection is always possible. At the same time as touch loses its sensorial, sensual value for us ("touching is an interaction of the senses rather than a simple contact of an object with the skin"), it is possible that it returns as the strategy of a universe of communication—but as the field of *tactile* and *tactical* simulation, where the message becomes "massage," tentacular solicitation, test. Everywhere you're tested, palpated, the method is "tactical," the sphere of communication is "tactile." Without even speaking of the ideology of "contact," that is being pushed in all its forms as a substitute for social rapport, there is an entire social configuration that orbits around the test (the question/answer cell) as around the commandments of the molecular code.

The political sphere entirely loses its specificity when it enters into the game of the media and public opinion polls, that is to say into the sphere of the integrated circuit of question/ answer. The electoral sphere is in any case the first great institution where social exchange is reduced to obtaining an answer. It is due to this sign-simplification that it is the first one to become universal. Universal suffrage is the first of the mass-media. All through the 19th and 20th centuries political and economic practice merge increasingly into the same type of discourse. Propaganda and advertising fuse in the same marketing and merchandising of objects and ideologies. This convergence of language between the economic and the political is furthermore what marks a society such as ours, where "political economy" is fully realized. It is also by the same token its end, since the two spheres are abolished in an entirely separate reality, or hyperreality, which is that of the media. There, too, there is an elevation of each term to a greater power, that of the third-order simulacra.

"That many regret the 'corruption' of politics by the media, deploring that TV and public opinion polls have replaced so quickly the formation of opinion, shows only that they understand nothing about politics."

What is characteristic of this phase of political hyperrealism is the necessary conjunction between the bipartite system and the entry into the play of the polls as mirror of this alternating equivalence of the political game.

The polls are located in a dimension beyond all social *production*. They refer only to a simulacrum of public opinion. A mirror of opinion analogous in its way to that of the Gross National Product: imaginary mirror of the productive forces, without regard to their social ends or lack thereof. What is essential is only that "it" reproduces itself. The same as for public opinion: what is essential is that it shadow itself incessantly in its own image. Therein lies the secret of mass representation. It is no longer necessary that anyone *produce* an opinion, all that is needed is that all *reproduce* public opinion, in the sense that all opinions get caught up in this kind of general equivalent, and once more proceed from it (reproduce it, whatever they make of it, on the level of individual choice). For opinions as for material goods: production is dead, long live reproduction.

If McLuhan's formula makes any sense it is certainly in this connection. [4] Public opinion is *par excellence* at the same time medium and message. And the polls that inform it are the incessant imposition of the medium as message. In this sense they are of the same nature as TV and the electronic media, which we have seen are also only a perpetual game of question/answer, an instrument of perpetual polling.

The polls manipulate *that which cannot be*

decided. Do they really affect the vote? True, false? Do they give an exact picture of reality, or simple tendencies, or the refraction of this reality in a hyperspace of simulation whose curve even is unknown? True, false, undecidable. Their most sophisticated analyses leave room always for the reversibility of the hypotheses. Statistics is only casuistry. This undecidable quality is proper to any process of simulation (see above, the crisis of indecision). The internal logic of these procedures (statistics, probability, operational cybernetics) is certainly rigorous and "scientific"; somehow though it does not stick, it is a fabulous fiction whose index of refraction in any reality (true or false) is nil. This is even what gives these *models* their forcefulness. But also it is this which only leaves them, as truth, the paranoid projection tests of a case, or of a group which dreams of a miraculous correspondance of the real to their models, and therefore of an absolute manipulation.

What is true of the statistics scenario is also true of the regulated partition of the political sphere: the alternation of the forces in power, majority/minority, substitutive, etc. On this limit of pure representation, "that" no longer represents anything. Politics die of the too-well-regulated game of distinctive oppositions. The political sphere (and that of power in general) becomes empty. This is somehow the payment for the accomplishing of the political class' desire: that of a perfect manipulation of social representation. Surreptitiously and silently, all social substance has left this machine in the very moment of its perfect reproduction.

The same thing holds true for the polls. The only ones who believe in them finally are the members of the political class, just as the only ones who really believe in advertising and market studies are the marketeers and advertisers. This is not because they are particularly stupid (though that we can't exclude either) but because the polls are homogenous with the current functioning of politics. They take on a "real" tactical value, they come into play as a factor in the regulation of the political class according to its own rules of the game. It therefore has reason to believe in them, and it believes. But who else does, really? It is the political class' burlesque spectacle, hyper-representative of nothing at all, that people taste by way of the polls and media. There is a jubilation proper to spectacular nullity, and the last form it takes is that of *statistical contemplation*. This is accompanied always, we know, by a profound disappointment—the kind of disillusion that the polls provoke in absorbing so utterly the public's voice, in short-circuiting all process of expression. The fascination they exercise is in accordance with this neutralization by emptiness, with this trance they create by anticipation of the image over all possible reality.

The problem of the polls is not at all that of their objective influence. Just as for propaganda or publicity, their influence is negated by individual or collective inertia or resistance. The problem is the operational simulation that they institute over the entire spectrum of social practices: that of the progressive *leucemiazation* of all social substance, that is the substitution for blood of the white lymph of media.

The question/answer cycle finds extension in all domains. You slowly find that the entire realm of inquiries, polls, and statistics needs to be looked at again in relation to this radical suspicion which falls upon their methods. But the selfsame suspicion falls on ethnology. Unless you admit that the natives are perfect naturals, incapable of simulation, the problem is the same as here: the impossibility of obtaining for a *directed* question any answer other than *simulated* (other than reproducing the question). It isn't even certain that you can interrogate plants, animals, nor even inert matter in the exact sciences with any chance of "objective" response. As to the response of the polled to the poll-takers, the natives to the ethnologist, the analyzed to the analyst, you can be sure that the circularity is total: the ones questioned always pretend to be as the question imagines and solicits them to be. Even psychoanalytic transference and counter-transference fall today under the sway of this stimulated, simulated-anticipated response, which is none other than the very model of the self-fulfilling prophecy. [5] We come then upon a strange paradox: the word of the polled, the analyzed, the natives, is irremediably short-circuited and lost, and it is on the basis of this foreclosure that these respective disciplines— ethnology, psychoanalysis, sociology—are going to be able to experience such marvelous growth. But they become puffed-up on mere wind, for it is in that respect that the circular response of the polled, the analyzed, the natives is all the same a challenge and a triumphant revenge. It is that they place the spotlight back on the question itself, isolate it in offering it the mirror of the answer it was awaiting, and show it helpless to ever quit the vicious circle which in fact is that of power. Just as in the electoral system, in which the representatives no longer represent anything because they control so well the responses of the electoral body. But everything has, somehow, eluded the ruling class' grasp. This is why the dominated answer of the natives is all the same a real response, a desperate vengeance: that of letting power bury power.

The "advanced democratic" systems are stabilized on the formula of bipartite alternation. The monopoly in fact remains that of a homogenous political class, from left to right, but it must not be exercised as such. The one-party totalitarian regime is an unstable form—it defuses the political scene, it no longer assures the feed-back of public opinion, the minimal flux in the integrated circuit which constitutes the transistorized poitical machine. Alternation, on the other hand, is the end of the end of representation, so solicitation is maximal, by dint of simple formal constraint, when you are approaching most nearly a perfect competitive equation between the two parties. This is logical. Democracy realizes the law of equivalence in the political order. This law is accomplished in the back-and-forth movement of the two terms which reactivates their equivalence but allows, by the minute difference, a public consensus to be formed and the cycle of representation to be closed. Operational theatre, where the only play staged anymore is the fulginous reflection of political Reason. The "free choice" of individuals, which is the credo of democracy, leads in fact precisely to the opposite: the vote becomes functionally *obligatory*: if it is not legally, it is by statistical constraint, the structure of alternation, reinforced by the polls. [6] The vote becomes functionally *aleatory*: when democracy attains an advanced formal stage, it distributes itself around equal quotients (50/50). The vote comes to resemble a Brownian movement of particles or the calculation of probabilities. It is as if everyone voted by chance, or monkeys voted.

At this point it makes no difference at all what the parties in power are expressing historically and socially. It is *necessary* even that they represent nothing: the fascination of the game, the polls, the formal and statistical compulsion of the game is all the greater.

"Classical" universal suffrage already implies a certain neutralization of the political field, if only by the consensus on the rules of the game. But you can still distinguish therein the representatives from the represented, on the basis of a real social antagonism of opinion. It is the neutralization of this contradictory referent, under the sign of a public opinion from now on equal unto itself, mediated and homogenized by anticipation (the polls) that will make alternation possible "at the top": simulation of opposition between two parties, absorption of their respective objectives, reversibility of the entire discourse one into the other. It is, beyond the representing and the represented, the pure form of representation—just as simulation characterizes, beyond the signifier and the signified, the pure form of the political economy of the sign—exactly as the floating of currency and its countable relations characterizes, beyond use and exchange value, beyond all substance of production, the pure form of value.

It might appear that the historical movement of capital carries it from one open competition towards oligopoly, then towards monopoly—that the democratic movement goes from multiple parties toward bipartism, then toward the single party. Nothing of the sort: oligopoly, or the current duopoly results from a *tactical doubling of monopoly*. In all domains duopoly is the final stage of monopoly. It is not the public will (state intervention, anti-trust laws, etc.) which breaks up the monopoly of the market—it is the fact that any unitary system, if it wishes to survive, must acquire a *binary regulation*. This changes nothing as far as monopoly is concerned. On the contrary, power is absolute only if it is capable of diffraction into various equivalents, if it knows how to take off so as to put more on. This goes for brands of soap-suds as well as peaceful co-existence. You need two superpowers to keep the universe under control: a single empire would crumble of itself. And the equilibrium of terror alone can allow a regulated opposition to be established, for the strategy is structural, never atomic. This regulated opposition can furthermore be ramified into a more complex scenario. The matrix remains binary. It will never again be a matter of a duel or open competitive struggle, but of couples of simultaneous opposition.

From the smallest disjunctive unity (question/answer particle) up to the great alternating systems that control the economy, politics, world co-existence, the matrix does not change: it is always the 0/1, the binary scansion that is affirmed as the metastable or homeostatic form of the current systems. This is the nucleus of the simulation processes which dominate us. It can be organized as a play of unstable variations, from polyvalence to tautology, without threatening the strategic bipolar form: it is the divine form of simulation.

Why are there *two* towers at New York's World Trade Center? All of Manhattan's great buildings were always happy enough to affront each other in a competitive verticality, the result of which is an architectural panorama in the image of the capitalist system: a pyramidal jungle, all the buildings attacking each other. The system profiled itself in a celebrated image that you had of New York when you arrived there by boat. This image has completely changed in the last few years. The effigy of the capitalist system has passed from the pyramid to the perforated card. Buildings are no longer obelisks, but lean one upon the other, no longer suspicious one of the other, like columns in a statistical graph. This new architecture incarnates a system that is no longer competitive, but compatible, and where competition has disappeared for the benefit of the correlations. (New York is the world's only city therefore that retraces all along its history, and with a prodigious fidelity and in all its scope, the actual form of the capitalistic system—it changes instantly in function of the latter. No European city does so.) This architectural graphism is that of the monopoly; the two W.T.C. towers, perfect parallelepipeds a ¼-mile high on a square base, perfectly balanced and blind communicating vessels. The fact that there are two of them *signifies* the end of all competition, the end of all original reference. Paradoxically, if there were only one, the monopoly would not be incarnated, because we have seen how it stabilizes on a dual form. For the sign to be pure, it has to duplicate itself: it is the duplication of the sign which destroys its meaning. This is what Andy Warhol demonstrates also: the multiple replicas of Marilyn's face are there to show at the same time the death of the original and the end of representation. The two towers of the W.T.C. are the visible sign of the closure of the system in a vertigo of duplication, while the other skyscrapers are each of them the original moment of a system constantly transcending itself in a perpetual crisis and self-challenge.

There is a particular fascination in this reduplication. As high as they are, higher than all the others, the two towers signify nevertheless the end of verticality. They ignore the other buildings, they are not of the same race, they no longer challenge them, nor compare themselves to them, they look one into the other as into a mirror and culminate in this prestige of similitude. What they project is the idea of the model that they are one for the other, and their twin altitude presents no longer any value of transcendence. They signify only that the strategy of models and commutations wins out in the very heart of the system itself—and New York is really the heart of it—over the traditional strategy of competition. The buildings of Rockefeller Center still direct their gaze one at the other into their glass or steel facades, in the city's infinite specularity. The towers, on the other hand, are blind, and no longer have a facade. All referential of habitat, of the facade as face, of interior and exterior, that you still find in the Chase Manhattan or in the boldest mirror-buildings of the 60's, is erased. At the same time as the rhetoric of verticality, the rhetoric of the mirror has disappeared. There remains only a series closed on the number two, just as if architecture, in the image of the system, proceeded only from an unchangeable genetic code, a definitive model.

The Hyperrealism of Simulation

All of this defines a digital space, a magnetic field for the code, with polarizations, diffractions, gravitations of the models and always, always, the flux of the smallest disjunctive unities (the question/answer cell, that is like the cybernetic atom of meaning). We should compare this kind of control with the traditional repressive space, the police-space that still corresponded to a *signifying* violence. Space of reactionary conditioning that took its inspiration from the total Pavlovian disposition of programmed, repetitive aggressions, and which you find again multiplied in scale in "hard sell" advertising and in the political propaganda of the 1930's. Raw industrial violence, aiming to induce behaviors of terror and of animal obeisance. All of that no longer has any meaning. The totalitarian, bureaucratic concentration is a scheme which dates from the era of the mercantile law of value. The system of equivalences imposes in effect the form of a general equivalent, and therefore the centralization of a global process. Archaic rationality compared to that of simulation; there is no longer a single general equivalent, but a diffraction of models that plays a regulatory role. No longer the form of the general equivalent, but that of distinctive opposition. From injunction you pass to disjunction by the code, from the ultimatum you pass to the solicitation, from the required passivity to models constructed all at once on the basis of the "active response" of the subject, on its implication, its "ludic" participation, etc., towards a total environmental model made out of incessant spontaneous responses of joyous feed-back and irradiating contact. This is the "concretization of the general atmosphere," according to Nicolas Schöffer, the great festival of Participation, made out of myriads of stimuli, miniaturized tests, infinitely divisible question/answers, all magnetized by a few great models in the luminous field of the code.

Here comes the time of the great Culture of tactile communication, under the sign of the technico-luminous cinematic space of total spatio-dynamic theatre.

This is a completely imaginary contact-world of sensorial mimetics and tactile mysticism; it is essentially an entire ecology that is grafted on this universe of operational simulation, multistimulation and multiresponse. We naturalize this incessant test of successful adaptation in assimilating it into animal mimesis. "The adaptation of animals to the colors and forms of their milieu is a valid phenomenon for man" (Nicolas Schöffer), and the same for Indians, with their "innate sense of ecology"! Tropisms, mimetics, empathy: the complete ecological Evangel of open systems, with positive or negative feedback, is going to rush into this breech, with an ideology of regulation by information which is only the avatar, according to a more flexible rationality, of Pavlov's reflex. So it is that we graduate from electro-shock therapy to bodily expression as a means of conditioning mental health. Everywhere the disposition of force and forcing yield to dispositions of ambiance, with operationalization of the notions of need, perception, desire, etc. Generalized ecology, mystique of the "niche" and of the context, milieu-simulation right up to "Centers of Esthetic and Cultural Re-Animation" foreseen in the VIIth Plan (why not?) and Center of Sexual Leisure, constructed in the form of a breast, that will offer a "superior euphoria due to a pulsating ambiance. . . . The workers from all classes will be able to penetrate into these stimulating centers." Spatiodynamic fascination, like this "total theatre" established "according to a hyperbolic circular disposition turning around a cylindrical cone": no more scene, cut-off point, or "regard": end of the spectacle as well as of the spectacular, towards the total environmental, fused together, tactile, esthesia and no longer esthetics, etc. We can think of the total theatre of Artaud only with black humor, his Theatre of Cruelty, of which this spatiodynamic simulaton is only an abject caricature. Here cruelty is replaced by "minimal and maximal stimulus thresholds," by the invention of "perceptive codes calculated on the basis of saturation thresholds." Even the good old "catharsis" of the classical theatre of the passions has become today homeopathy by simulation. So goes creativity.

This also means the collapse of reality into hyperrealism, in the minute duplication of the real, preferably on the basis of another reproductive medium—advertising, photo, etc. From medium to medium the real is volatilized;

it becomes an allegory of death, but it is reinforced by its very destruction; it becomes the real for the real, fetish of the lost object—no longer object of representation, but ecstasy of denegation and of its own ritual extermination: the hyperreal.

Realism had already begun this tendency. The rhetoric of the real already meant that the status of the latter had been gravely menaced (the golden age is that of language's innocence, where it doesn't have to add an "effect of reality" to what is said). Surrealism is still solidary with the realism it contests, but augments its intensity by setting it off against the imaginary. The hyperreal represents a much more advanced phase, in the sense that even this contradiction between the real and the imaginary is effaced. The unreal is no longer that of dream or of fantasy, of a beyond or a within, it is that of a *hallucinatory resemblance of the real with itself.* To exist from the crisis of representation, you have to lock the real up in pure repetition. Before emerging in pop art and pictorial neo-realism, this tendency is at work already in the new novel. The project is already there to empty out the real, extirpate all psychology, all subjectivity, to move the real back to pure objectivity. In fact this objectivity is only that of the pure look—objectivity at last liberated from the object, that is nothing more than the blind relay station of the look which sweeps over it. Circular seduction where you can detect easily the unconscious desire of no longer being visible at all.

This is certainly the impression that the new novel leaves: this rage for eliding sense in a minute and blind reality. Syntax and semantics have disappeared—there is no longer apparition, but instead subpoena of the object, severe interrogation of its scattered fragments— neither metaphor nor metonymy: successive immanence under the policing structure of the look. This "objective" minuteness arouses a vertigo of reality, a vertigo of death on the limits of representation-for-the-sake-of-represent-ation. End of the old illusions of relief, perspective and depth (spatial and psychological) bound to the perception of the object: it is the entire optic, the view become operational on the surface of things, it is the look become molecular code of the object.

Several modalities of this vertigo of realistic simulation are possible:

Jean Baudrillard

I. The deconstruction of the real into details—closed paradigmatic declension of the object—flattening, linearity and seriality of the partial objects.

II. The endlessly reflected vision: all the games of duplication and reduplication of the object in detail. This multiplication is presented as a deepening, that is for a critial metalanguage, and it was doubtless true in a reflexive configuration of the sign, in a dialectic of the mirror. From now on, though, this indefinite refraction is only another type of seriality. The real is no longer reflected, instead it feeds off itself till the point of emaciation.

III. The properly serial form (Andy Warhol). Here not only the syntagmatic dimension is abolished, but the paradigmatic as well. Since there no longer is any formal flection or even internal reflection, but contiguity of the same—flection and reflection zero. Like those two twin sisters in a dirty picture: the charnel reality of their bodies is erased by the resemblance. How to invest your energies in one, when her beauty is immediately duplicated by the other? The regard can go only from one to the other, all vision is locked into this coming-and-going. Subtle way of murdering the original, but also singular seduction, where all attention to the object is intercepted by its infinite diffraction into itself (inverted scenario of the Platonic myth of the reunion of the separated halves of the symbol—here the sign multiplies like protozoans). This seduction is possibly that of death, in the sense that for sexual beings, death is possibly not nothingness, but simply the mode of reproduction anterior to the sexual. This generation by model along an endless chain that in effect recalls the protozoans and is opposed to a sexual mode that we tend, inaccurately, to confuse with life itself.

IV. But this pure mechanization is doubtless only a paradoxical limit: the true generating formula, that which englobes all the others, and which is somehow the stabilized form of the code, is that of binarity, of digitality. Not pure repetition, but the minimal separation, the least amount of inflection between the two terms, that is to say the "very smallest common paradigm" that the fiction of sense could possibly support. Combination of differentiation internal to the pictorial object and to the object of consummation, this simulation retreats in contemporary art to be no more than the minute difference that still separates the hyperreal from hyperpainting. The latter pretends to extend right up to a sacrificial effacement before the real, but you know how all these prestigious elements in painting resuscitate in this minute difference: all of painting takes refuge in the border that separates the painted surface and the wall. And in the signature: metaphysical sign of painting and of the whole metaphysic of representation, at the limit where it takes itself for model (the "pure look") and turns back upon itself in the compulsive repetition of the code.

The very definition of the real becomes: *that of which it is possible to give an equivalent reproduction.* This is contemporaneous with a science that postulates that a process can be perfectly reproduced in a set of given conditions, and also with the industrial rationality that postulates a universal system of equivalency (classical representation is not equivalence, it is transcription, interpretation, commentary). At the limit of this process of reproductibility, the real is not only what can be reproduced, but *that which is always already reproduced.* The hyperreal.

And so: end of the real, and end of art, by total absorption one into the other? No:

hyperrealism is the limit of art, and of the real, by respective exchange, on the level of the simulacrum, of the privileges and the prejudices which are their basis. The hyperreal transcends representation (cf. J.F. Lyotard, *L'Art Vivant*, number on hyperrealism) only because it is entirely in simulation. The tourniquet of representation tightens madly, but of an implosive madness, that, far from eccentric (marginal) inclines towards the center to its own infinite repetition. Analogous to the distancing characteristic of the dream, that makes us say that we are only dreaming; but this is only the game of censure and of perpetuation of the dream. Hyperrealism is made an integral part of a coded reality that it perpetuates, and for which it changes nothing.

In fact, we should turn our definition of hyperrealism inside out: *It is reality itself today that is hyperrealist.* Surrealism's secret already was that the most banal reality could become surreal, but only in certain privileged moments that nevertheless are still connected with art and the imaginary. Today it is quotidian reality in its entirety—political, social, historical and economic—that from now on incorporates the simulatory dimension of hyperrealism. We live

147

everywhere already in an "esthetic" hallucination of reality. The old slogan "truth is stranger than fiction," that still corresponded to the surrealist phase of this estheticization of life, is obsolete. There is no more fiction that life could possibly confront, even victoriously—it is reality itself that disappears utterly in the game of reality— radical disenchantment, the cool and cybernetic phase following the hot stage of fantasy.

It is thus that for guilt, anguish and death there can be substituted the total joy of the signs of guilt, despair, violence and death. It is the very euphoria of simulation, that sees itself as the abolition of cause and effect, the beginning and the end, for all of which it substitutes reduplication. In this manner all closed systems protect themselves at the same time from the referential—as well as from all metalanguage that the system forestalls in playing at its own metalanguage; that is to say in duplicating itself in its own critique of itself. In simulation, the metalinguistic illusion duplicates and completes the referential illusion (pathetic hallucination of the sign and pathetic hallucination of the real).

"It's a circus," "It's theatre," "It's a movie," old adages, old naturalistic denunciation. These sayings are now obsolete. The problem now is

that of the *satellization of the real*, the putting into
orbit of an indefinable reality without common
measure to the fantasies that once used to orna-
ment it. This satellization we find further naturalized in the two-rooms-kitchen shower that
they have launched into orbit—to the powers of
space, you could say—with the last lunar module.
The banality of the earthly habitat lifted to the
rank of cosmic value, of absolute decor—hypostatized in space—this is the end of metaphysics,
the era of hyperreality that begins. [8] But the
spatial transcendence of the banality of the two-
rooms, like its cool and mechanical figuration of
hyperrealism, [9] says only one thing: that this
module, such as it is, participates in a
hyperspace of representation—where each is
already technically in possession of the instantaneous reproduction of his own life, where the
pilots of the Tupolev that crashed at Bourget
could see themselves die live on their own
camera. This is nothing else that the short-
circuit of the response by the question in the
test, instantaneous process of re-conduction
whereby reality is immediately contaminated
by its simulacrum.

There used to be, before, a specific class of
allegorical and slightly diabolical objects: mir-

rors, images, works of art (concepts?)—
simulacra, but transparent and manifest (you
didn't confuse the counterfeit with the original),
that had their characteristic style and savoir-
faire. And pleasure consisted then rather in
discovering the "natural" in what was artificial
and counterfeit. Today, when the real and the
imaginary are confused in the same operational
totality, the esthetic fascination is everywhere.
It is a subliminal perception (a sort of sixth
sense) of deception, montage, scenaria—of the
overexposed reality in the light of the models—
no longer a production space, but a reading
strip, strip of coding and decoding, magnetized
by the signs—esthetic reality—no longer by the
premeditation and the distance of art, but by its
elevation to the second level, to the second
power, by the anticipation and the immanence
of the code. A kind of non-intentional parody
hovers over everything, of technical simulation,
of indefinable fame to which is attached an
esthetic pleasure, that very one of reading and
of the rules of the game. Travelling of signs, the
media, of fashion and the models, of the blind
and brilliant ambiance of the simulacra.

A long time ago art prefigured this turning
which is that today of daily life. Very quickly the

work turns back on itself as the manipulation of the signs of art: over-signification of art, "academism of the signifier," as Levi-Strauss would say, who interprets it really as the form-sign. It is then that art enters into its indefinite *reproduction*: all that reduplicates itself, even if it be the everyday and banal reality, falls by the token under the sign of art, and becomes esthetic. It's the same thing for production, which you could say is entering today this esthetic reduplication, this phase when, expelling all content and finality, it becomes somehow abstract and non-figurative. It expresses then the pure form of production, it takes upon itself, as art, the value of a finality without purpose. Art and industry can then exchange their signs. Art can become a reproducing machine (Andy Warhol), without ceasing to be art, since the machine is only a sign. And production can lose all social finality so as to be verified and exalted finally in the prestigious, hyperbolic signs that are the great industrial combines, the ¼-mile-high towers or the number mysteries of the GNP.

And so art is everywhere, since artifice is at the very heart of reality. And so art is dead, not only because its critical transcendence is gone, but because reality itself, entirely impregnated by an aesthetic which is inseparable from its own structure, has been confused with its own image. Reality no longer has the time to take on the appearance of reality. It no longer even surpasses fiction: it captures every dream even before it takes on the appearance of a dream. Schizophrenic vertigo of these serial signs, for which no counterfeit, no sublimation is possible, immanent in their repetition—who could say what the reality is that these signs simulate? They no longer even repress anything (which is why, if you will, simulation pushes us close to the sphere of psychosis). Even the primary processes are abolished in them. The cool universe of digitality has absorbed the world of metaphor and metonymy. The principle of simulation wins out over the reality principle just as over the principle of pleasure.

Translated by Philip Beitchman

Notes

1. Counterfeit and reproduction imply always an anguish, a disquieting foreignness: the uneasiness before the photograph, considered like a witches trick—and more generally before any technical apparatus, which is always an apparatus of reproduction, is related by Benjamin to the uneasiness before the mirror-image. There is already sorcery at work in the mirror. But how much more so when this image can be detached from the mirror and be transported, stocked, reproduced at will (cf. *The Student of Prague*, where the devil detaches the image of the student from the mirror and harrasses him to death by the intermediary of this image). All reproduction implies therefore a kind of black magic, from the fact of being seduced by one's own image in the water, like Narcissus, to being haunted by the double and, who knows, to the mortal turning back of this vast technical apparatus secreted today by man as his own image (the narcissistic mirage of technique, McLuhan) and that returns to him, cancelled and distorted—endless reproduction of himself and his power to the limits of the world. Reproduction is diabolical in its very essence; it makes something fundamental vacillate. This has hardly changed for us: simulation (that we describe here as the operation of the code) is still and always the place of a gigantic enterprise of manipulation, of control and of death, just like the imitative object (primitive statuette, image of photo) always had as objective an operation of black image.

2. There is furthermore in Monod's book a flagrant contradiction, which reflects the ambiguity of all current science. His discourse concerns the code, that is the third-order simulacra, but it does so still according to "scientific" schemes of the second-order—objectiveness, "scientific" ethic of knowledge, science's principle of truth and transcendence. All things incompatible with the indeterminable models of the third-order.

3. "It's the feeble 'definition' of TV which condemns its spectator to rearranging the few points retained into a kind of *abstract work*. He participates suddenly in the creation of a reality that was only just presented to him in dots: the television watcher is in the position of an individual who is asked to project his own fantasies on inkblots that are not supposed to represent anything." TV as perpetual Rorschach test. And furthermore: "The TV image requires each instant that we 'close' the spaces in the mesh by a convulsive sensuous participation that is profoundly kinetic and tactile."

4. "The Medium is the Message" is the very slogan of the poitical economy of the sign, when it enters into the third-order simulation—the distinction between the medium and the message characterizes instead signification of the second-order.

5. The entire current "psychological" situation is characterized by this short-circuit.

Doesn't emancipation of children and teenagers, once the initial phase of revolt is passed and once there has been established the *principle* of the *right* to emancipation, seem like the *real* emancipation of parents. And the young (students, high-schoolers, adolescents) seem to sense it in their always more insistent demand (though still as paradoxical) for the presence and advice of parents or of teachers. Alone at last, free and responsible, it seemed to them suddenly that other people possibly have absconded with their true liberty. Therefore, there is no question of "leaving them be." They're going to hassle them, not with any emotional or material spontaneous demand, but with an exigency that has been premeditated and corrected by an implicit oedipal knowledge. Hyperdependence (much greater than before) distorted by irony and refusal, *parody of libidinous original mechanisms*. Demand without content, without referent, unjustified, but for all that all the more severe—naked demand with no possible answer. The contents of knowledge (teaching) or of affective relations, the pedagogical or familial referent having been eliminated in the act of emancipation, there remains only a demand linked to the empty form of the institution—perverse demand, and for that reason all the more obstinate. "Transferable" desire (that is to say non-referential, un-referential), desire that has been fed by lack, by the.place left vacant, "liberated," desire captured in its own vertiginous image, desire of desire, as pure form, hyperreal. Deprived of symbolic substance, it doubles back upon itself, draws its energy from its own reflection and its disappointment with itself. This is literally today the "demand," and it is obvious that unlike the "classical" objective or transferable relations this one here is insoluble and interminable.

Simulated Oedipus.

Francois Richard: "Students asked to be seduced either bodily or verbally. But also they are aware of this

Jean Baudrillard

and they play the game, ironically. 'Give us your knowledge, your presence, you have the word, speak, you are there for that.' Contestation certainly, but not only: the more authority is contested, vilified, the greater the need for authority as such. They play at Oedipus also, to deny it all the more vehemently. The 'teach', he's Daddy, they say; it's fun, you play at incest, malaise, the untouchable, at being a tease—in order to de-sexualize finally." Like one under analysis who asks for Oedipus back again, who tells the "oedipal" stories, who has the "analytical" dreams to satisfy the supposed request of the analyst, or to resist him? In the same way the student goes through his oedipal number, his seduction number, gets chummy, close, approaches, dominates—but this isn't desire, it's simulation. Oedipal psychodrama of simulation (neither less real nor less dramatic for all that). Very different from the real libidinal stakes of knowledge and power or even of a real mourning for the absence of same (as could have happened after '68 in the universities) Now we've reached the phase of desperate reproduction, and where the stakes are nil, the simulacrum is maximal—exacerbated and parodied simulation at one and the same time—as interminable as psychoanalysis and for the same reasons.

The interminable psychoanalysis.

There is a whole chapter to add to the history of transference and countertransference: that of their liquidation by simulation, of the impossible psycho-analysis because it is itself, from now on, that produces and reproduces the unconscious as its institutional substance. Psychoanalysis dies also of the exchange of the

156

signs of the unconscious. Just as revolution dies of the exchange of the critical signs of political economy. This short-circuit was well known to Freud in the form of the gift of the analytic dream, or with the "uninformed" patients, in the form of the gift of their analytic knowledge. But this was still interpreted as resistance, as detour, and did not put fundamentally into question either the process of analysis or the principle of transference. It is another thing entirely when the unconscious itself, the discourse of the unconscious becomes unfindable—according to the same scenario of simulative anticipation that we have seen at work on all levels with the machines of the third order. The analysis then can no longer end, it becomes logically and historically interminable, since it stabilizes on a puppet-substance of reproduction, an unconscious programmed on demand—an impossible-to-break-through point around which the whole analysis is rearranged. The messages of the unconscious have been short-circuited by the psycho-analysis "medium." This is libidinal hyperrealism. To the famous categories of the real, the symbolic and the imaginary, it is going to be necessary to add the hyperreal, which captures and obstructs the functioning of the three orders.

6. Athenian democracy, much more advanced than our own, had reached the point where the vote was considered as payment for a service, after all other repressive solutions had been tried and found wanting in order to insure a quorum.

7. In this sense we should radically criticize the projection that Levi-Strauss makes of binary structures

as "anthropological" mental structures and of dual organization as the basic structure of primitive society. The dualist form that Levi-Srauss would so love to apply to primitive society is never anything less than *our* own structural logic. Our very own code, that selfsame one that we use to dominate the "archaic" societies. Levi-Strauss has the kindness to slip this to them under the guise of mental structures that are common to the whole human race. They will thereby be better prepared to receive the baptism of the Occident.

8. The coefficient of reality is proportional to the imaginary in reverse which gives it is specific density. This is true of geographical and spatial exploration also. When there is no more territory virgin and therefore available for the imaginary, when the map covers the whole territory, then something like a principle of reality disappears. The conquest of space constitutes in this sense an irreversible threshold in the direction of the loss of the eartly referential. This is precisely the hemorrhage of reality as internal coherence of a limited universe when its limits retreat infinitely. The conquest of space follows that of the planet as the same fantastic enterprise of extending the jurisdiction of the real—to carry for example the flag, the technique, and the two-rooms-and-kitchen to the moon—same tentative to substantiate the concepts or to territorialize the unconscious—the latter equals making the human race unreal, or to reversing it into a hyperreality of simulation.

9. Or that of the metal-plated caravan or supermarket dear to hyperrealists, or Campbell's Soup dear to Andy Warhol, or the Mona Lisa, since she too has been

satellized around the planet, as absolute model of earthly art, no longer a work of art but a planetary simulacrum where everyone comes to witness himself (really his own death) in the gaze of the future.